HOW TO READ ANY MAN'S MIND

by

SERVET HASAN

authorHOUSE

1663 LIBERTY DRIVE, SUITE 200
BLOOMINGTON, INDIANA 47403
(800) 839-8640
www.authorhouse.com

First published by AuthorHouse 07/16/04

ISBN: 1-4184-3753-0 (e)
ISBN: 1-4184-3752-2 (sc)
ISBN: 1-4184-3751-4 (dj)

Library of Congress Control Number: 2004094007

Printed in the United States of America
Bloomington, Indiana

This book is printed on acid-free paper.

To Sabrina, the most perfect gift from God. You came to me wrapped in joy and laughter and tied together with a golden ribbon of love. I hope you never forget where you came from. I never will. All I have to do is look into your eyes, and I see His light shining through. It is my wish that you soar above the limits of the world, for that is where Earth touches Heaven and His power becomes your own. My arms will forever be your shelter, my heart your home. Be safe. I love you. −Mom

"How do I know the ways of all things at the Beginning?
By what is within me."
– Lao Tzu

TABLE OF CONTENTS

INTRODUCTION

"I can't believe the guy turned out to be such a jerk! Why didn't I see it coming? The signs were right there in front on me."

How many times have you said something similar to yourself? If you're anything like me, the answer is probably more times than you care to remember, or admit. I didn't understand how I could possibly date that many losers. What was I doing wrong? Why did I keep repeating the same mistake over and over and over again? They all looked like such nice guys. I couldn't figure it out.

Until one day, someone (my mother of all people) ever so politely pointed out that I didn't just attract these men; I voluntarily supplied them with my phone numbers—work, home, cell, my fax number for crying out loud! Countless numbers of heart-wrenching, bleed-all-over-myself disappointments may finally have paid off. How? The inner voice inside of me let out a scream that went something like, "Wake up, you idiot! If you opened your eyes and ears, you could have avoided all of this pain and heartache."

From the minute a man enters a room, everything about him is telling you something. His face alone is a virtual neon marquee of a hidden agenda. But sometimes it's a feeling that unlocks the key to a corner of their soul. By utilizing both forms of data, we can literally enter a man's mind. Impossible? Absolutely not. You already own the ability, whether you are conscious of it or not. How many times have you described yourself as having "a gut feeling," or "one of those hunches," about a certain someone, a certain situation? How many times have you said, "I trusted him from the minute I laid eyes on him," or, "I knew he was nothing but a liar," and been proven right? Likewise, haven't we all been subjected to somebody reacting to us for no apparent reason? Why does a person consciously choose not to call someone back or hire him or her for the job? Oftentimes the answer stems from an illogical explanation such as, "I just had a weird feeling about that guy. I don't know . . . something wasn't right." They just *knew*.

The majority of us read people every day. The trouble is, we don't know how to translate what's behind the patterns of behavior and use it to our advantage. Once you learn to define, clarify, and access this process at will, not only will you be able to pick up on the thoughts behind the words and interpret what is really being said but more importantly, what is *not* being said. Wouldn't it be nice to know if the man who said he'd call you later, meant it? Wouldn't it be nice to know if the man who said he loved you last night wasn't cheating on you today? Wouldn't it be nice to know if the person you hired wasn't going to turn into a flake once he got the job?

Whether you're considering dating, marrying, hiring, or working for someone, it's imperative that you learn how to distinguish between your allies and your adversaries. By avoiding the pitfalls that lead to bad decision making, you can not only enhance your relationships but also possibly save your life. Rapists don't wear signs. Muggers and murderers don't hand out business cards. Child molesters don't advertise. Every hour, an estimated 75 women are raped in the United States. Even more alarming is the fact that only 20% of female homicides are committed by strangers. The remaining 80% are people known by the victims—most of whom denied what they knew to be a potentially dangerous situation involving estranged husbands, boyfriends, and bad dates.

Predictability is actually the glue that bonds us together as human beings. Random acts of violence, referred to as occurring "out of the blue," or "all of a sudden," as if they were impossible to predict, are in reality the outcome of cause and effect, a process easily identifiable if (and that's a big if) you know what to look for. You will literally learn to look a man straight in the eye and, before he utters a single word, predict his intentions, be they harmful or not.

Not only that, but if you can read other people you can read how they read you. You can alter your personal style at the drop of a hat to project confidence, sincerity, and strength without appearing disingenuous or intimidating. Politicians do it all the time.

This is not a book about becoming a psychic. I will be the first to attest to the fact that there simply is no such thing, especially since for years I was told I was one. After decades of studying hundreds of psychics, I have yet to meet one that could accurately predict a person's future. At the same time, I have also been privileged to work with several spiritual leaders, all of whom have taught me that each and every one of us can master the ability to predict the outcome of our situations, our relationships, and our futures.

The magic is nothing more than the simple process of accessing our conscious and unconscious awareness simultaneously—and combining their forces. By becoming aware on both levels, we enter the world of foresight, what could be, instead of hindsight, what has been. The future is ours to own.

PART ONE

THE POWER OF INTUITION

"The really valuable thing is intuition." – Albert Einstein

CHAPTER ONE

FINDING FORESIGHT

Cathy turned and looked into the most incredible blue eyes she'd ever seen. So blue, she thought God had left behind a piece of the sky. "Let me help you with that," he said, reaching for one of the bags strung up her arm like plastic bracelets.

"Oh, I can handle it," she said flatly, not recognizing the stranger. "I've got it."

But as she uttered the words, one of the bags took a conspiratorial leap out of order and landed on the floor, spilling Gallo wine and a couple of Lean Cuisine dinners on the parking lot floor. She glanced down with a mixture of disgust and embarrassment. "Really, I can handle it."

"Oh, please," he insisted, shutting the trunk of the car for her. "There's no reason to pull that Ms. Independent crap with me."

Something about the condescending tone of his voice took her aback, her spine suddenly as rigid as a wire. But then this big, blond-haired, blue-eyed guy, who surely must have lived in the building in order to have been in the gated parking lot in the first place, got down on his hands and knees, sweeping up the errant items strewn across the garage floor.

"Thank you," she said, as he piled them into a bag. "I've got it from here."

"I think that's what you said before," he said, his voice softening to the texture of sandpaper rubbed across velvet. "Please, let me help you with that."

Cathy hesitated, and then shrugged her shoulders. "Well, if you just unlock the door."

"You know what, I was going to walk around, because I left my key at home," he replied, patting his pocket apologetically.

"Well, I'm going to have to find my key in that purse of mine. It could take forever," she explained, with a forced laugh. "I don't want to hold you up. Why don't you just go ahead and do that?"

"I'm not an axe murderer or anything. I'm just trying to be neighborly. So few people stop to help anymore. It's a shame."

Now she felt guilty. People always complained about how they didn't know their neighbors, especially in a city like Los Angeles. Could she have turned into one of those cynical, distrusting types? "I just didn't want to hold you up."

"Hey, I lost ten pounds eating those Lean Cuisines once. I just got out of college and had my first job. I was so stressed out that all I did was work, sleep, and eat. And eat, and eat. I'd come home at night and literally devour a whole quart of ice cream. I didn't know what else to do."

She smiled tentatively, still a bit nervous as she recovered the key from her purse and unlocked the door.

"Bet you can't guess the flavor?" he asked, shutting the security door behind them. "You're on the second floor, right?"

"Yes, I am."

He followed her up the stairs, still carrying the bag she insisted she could now handle on her own. "I thought I'd seen you throwing your trash out the other day."

"Probably." Cathy vacillated at her front door. "Thanks for all your help."

"No problem," he said, handing her the groceries. "But I didn't come this far only to stop at seeing you safely inside."

Once again, guilt crept in like a slow poison. Cathy smiled, while opening the door to her apartment. He seemed like such a nice guy. That was until he pushed the door open behind her, shoving her inside.

"Glad you see it my way," he said smugly.

Cathy knew something had gone wrong. She tried to speak, but she felt a sharp edge at the back of her throat, as if she'd been forced to swallow a knife.

What followed was an ordeal she thought she would never survive. For hours, he raped her, often threatening to cut her pretty face if she didn't cooperate. His mouth formed a tight, thin line, as if he might snap in two. Instinct warned her not to fight back. Later, she realized how lucky she was to be alive. Upon his capture, police informed Cathy that her assailant had stabbed three of his other victims, one of whom died.

Cathy learned the hard way that kindness is not a character trait. Being nice is something someone chooses to do, sometimes out of the goodness of their heart and sometimes for their own selfish and evil intentions.

Emily had only been divorced for a few months when she met him, this mysterious stranger who stared deep into her eyes. There was something dangerous about him, about his passion for living. A diehard romantic, he often whispered sweet nothings in her ear, telling her how he knew they were meant to be together, promising her that they would fulfill their destiny. He swept her off her feet.

Initially, everything seemed fine. He courted her in an old-fashioned manner, kissing her politely on the cheek before bidding her a good night. It didn't seem to matter that he always picked her up at her home and that they never went to his place (which was undergoing major renovations). It didn't seem to matter that he often ran low on cash, forcing her to pick up the check at restaurants or the movies. It didn't seem to matter that the trip they took to Hawaii ended up on her credit card. She had no clue what he was thinking. There wasn't a flicker behind those dark eyes. But like a shadow, he remained one step ahead of her, anticipating her every move. When she didn't check in, he questioned her whereabouts, determining which friends she could see and when—a trait she chalked up to his insecurity over losing her, instead of a desire to control her. She remained silent.

Until the tables turned. Suddenly, she could not reach him on anything but his cell phone. His eyes flashed back and forth when she questioned him, his shoulders rising when he explained that he wasn't easily accessible at work and that he spent little time at home while the house was under construction. His voice reached a high pitch at the end of sentences followed by evasive gestures and remarks. Still, a woman in love is a woman in love, and she believed him.

Six months and close to one hundred thousand dollars in debt later, she discovered that her dream man was married. He ripped her heart right down the seam.

They must have been watching Jennifer and Rick for some time, because they knew exactly what to look for—a very attractive couple at their bon voyage party before departing on an extended vacation to the Bahamas. They left before the guests to get to the ATM on the way to the airport so they'd have ample cash on hand, which they proudly announced to the majority of the patrons at the bar. Their friends wished them well, reminding them not to get in too much trouble.

Rick let Jenny in the car first, then walked around to the driver's side. But he stopped and searched the desolate parking lot before climbing inside.

"What is it?" she asked anxiously.

"Nothing." He shook his head uncertainly and started the car.

They drove approximately three blocks and pulled into the Bank of America parking lot. He left the engine running while he jumped out, bankcard stuck between his teeth while he pushed the other loose cards back into his wallet and shoved it into his back pocket.

Jenny shivered, her bones rising to the surface of her skin. Not sure why, she glanced into the side mirror of the car just in time to catch a glimpse of a man. She turned to look, knowing something was wrong, that he was too close to the car, and that he shouldn't be moving at her but away from her. In a split second, the flash of denim disappeared. Then the car door flew open and a man jumped in. He shoved something cold and hard into her head and ordered her not to move while he backed the car out of the parking spot just in time for her to see two other men approach her boyfriend with a gun.

After they took Rick's money, they beat him over the head with a tire iron, leaving him for dead. A bank employee found him in the same spot the following morning, unconscious but alive. Unfortunately, Jenny's ordeal lasted much longer. The man who abducted her stuffed her in the trunk of the car and drove her to an unknown destination. It seemed like it took hours to get there. By the time he got her to the motel, she was so dizzy that the world no longer spun on its axis. Yet, in that black aura of fear, Jenny found the presence of mind to remain calm. She waited until he went to the bathroom before she grabbed the keys and ran. Wrapped in nothing but a sheet, she made it to the motel office where she pounded on the door and the man let her in. He called the police.

The air was still murky and cold when Mandy decided to take an early morning run. Training for the marathon required discipline, and there was no reason to allow her conviction to drop with the temperature. Little did she know that this warranted being in the spotlight. Two to be precise. A car started to keep pace, lighting her way down the inky black asphalt. She heard the crunch of gravel beneath its wheels, the protesting purr of a restrained engine, and the electronic buzz of a window being lowered. A man called to her, shouting out names like baby, sugar, honey, and hot stuff, asking her to slow down because he knew what she wanted and would be happy to oblige her. Mandy's heart started beating faster, even before she broke into a run through the field, which she knew crossed over to the main part of town and an all night coffee shop.

But instead of the car pulling away, it stopped and she heard doors open and slam shut. Fog rolled in, but not enough to conceal her. "Hey, come on now, all we wanted to do is give you a ride. We're just trying to be friendly. You know . . . neighborly."

She didn't respond. The hair on the back of her neck stood on end. Something told her these men were not her friends.

When the heckling stopped, she knew she was in trouble. Mandy sensed the pain deep inside of them that made them want to hurt someone. In this case, her. They were running after her. Body heaving, barely able to see straight, she ran faster than she'd ever run before. So fast, the whole world seemed to speed up, and she reached the coffee shop in no time at all. No men were behind her as she pushed the doors open and stumbled inside. It took awhile for her breathing to return to normal. It stayed shallow and ragged, and made a funny noise, as if something had broken free inside and was rattling around inside of her. The men never showed up. Just the police.

A yellow sedan, the color of a smoker's tooth, stopped at an intersection just as thirteen-year-old Linda stepped off the sidewalk to cross the street. Smoke billowed from the cracked down window. The car didn't move as quickly as most cars would, which made Linda uneasy. Should she cross in front of it? Behind it? As she hesitated, the car door swung open and a man wearing a brown baseball cap and dark sunglasses pointed a gun at her head. "Get in the car," he demanded. "Or I'll kill you."

She didn't know what made her do it, except that her mother had repeatedly told her never to get in a car with a strange man, let alone a man with a gun. She figured she'd be better off dead, shot right there in the middle of a public intersection than to get in the car and be tortured and then shot. She took off running, screaming to anyone, and no one at all, "Call 911, call 911!"

The car made an abrupt u-turn and screeched away.

Despite the fact that John struck her as a bundle of contradictions—soft and hard, sour and sweet, sacred and profane—Susan hired the guy. She overlooked the fact that he hadn't stayed in a position longer than a year because he was "underutilized." He seemed so nice and honest when he edged toward her with smiles of sweet delight that, despite her better judgment, she hired the man. She felt she should give him a second chance, as he seemed genuinely interested in her future. Both she and her computer company didn't stand a digitalized prayer.

At first, he simply started showing up late for work. Then, he staged well-rehearsed lunches, disappearing for hours on end. Needless to say, he called in sick every Friday without fail. When Susan confronted him, he smirked and told her how much he valued her aiding him in finding his direction (which apparently was at a neighboring bar) and would prove it to her. After abusing their friendship further, she put her foot down and threatened to fire him. The next day, he "slipped" in the file room and filed for long-term disability.

Gina looked up at her husband, her face chalk white and drawn. "I'm getting a restraining order," she informed him defiantly. "So touch me again, and you'll have the police to deal with."

That's when his hands slid around her throat. Every breath she took was painful, the air hurting under the pressure. He didn't let up, pressing tighter into her, his face twisted with sheer pleasure. Fortuitously, the doorbell rang. Gina's son had forgotten his key and was banging and ringing happily to be let in. Her husband dropped her like a rag doll. But she didn't forget it, and shortly thereafter Gina moved in with a friend her husband couldn't possibly locate.

Later, Gina contacted the court and filed for a restraining order. The day of her hearing with the judge, her husband was waiting for her on the courthouse steps. He stabbed her fourteen times. She died instantly.

There are thousands of equally shocking scenarios similar to the ones mentioned above—with one exception. All of these horrendous stories happened to people I knew personally. I did not want the same mistakes repeated again with those I love, especially my own fourteen-year-old daughter.

How we choose to react to a situation can be life altering. Why then, if we have a doubt, do we choose to ignore it? Gut reactions give validity to the notion that there might be someone following you down an empty street, or that there might be something evil and harmful behind a seemingly innocent gesture a man makes. By the time you actually assess a situation your brain has done the bulk of the work. It's given you enough clues to guide you in the right direction. Each of the victims mentioned here initially had a feeling. For those in danger, fear rose in them so exorbitantly that none questioned the words that came swiftly, silently. "Run," or "Scream," or "Just be quiet and don't fight." Whether they chose an active approach, such as fight or flight, or a reactive response, in most cases it saved their lives.

Denial is dangerous. Conscious thought is even more insidious, as it hides relevant information from us based upon prejudices, preconceived judgments, and basic self-doubt. Whether we care to admit it or not, danger lurks around every corner. A murderer, a stalker, an estranged husband, a jealous boyfriend, or a serial rapist can be found in line with us at the grocery store, living next door to us, or working with us.

Must we all be subjected to such life threatening circumstances to fully comprehend the importance of our own perception? No. We don't. To believe that people's actions come out of nowhere is no more accurate than saying that our actions are not preceded by thoughts. Everything we say and do occurs twice. First in the mind, then in the implementation. Did these women see what was coming? Only in hindsight did they admit that they'd experienced an uneasy feeling, a feeling that something wasn't quite right.

Later, Jenny even went so far as to admit that she'd seen her abductor's car parked in the lot the day before, and found it somewhat suspicious.

We all own part of the miraculous ability to predict human behavior. Nature's greatest accomplishment resides within each and every one of us. Intuition. Before understanding physical nuances, take the time to learn about those that are not. Your life may depend upon it.

CHAPTER TWO

WHAT IS INTUITION?

Intuition is derived from the Latin root *in,* meaning the obvious, and *tueri,* which means to "look at." By definition then, intuition is the ability to look inward, to consciously connect with the subconscious mind. In other words, it's a cognitive process.

Again, this is not a "psychic" ability. Certainly, there are those who believe in psychics and their propensity to predict everything from marriages and illness, to your next career move. In most cases, they will attest to the fact that they "pick up" on a person's energy. If this were true, then even the most gifted medium would be highly unreliable, as energy is not solid or fixed but rather in constant motion. Most people spend the majority of their thinking time reconstructing themselves. Faced with new challenges daily, the decisions they impose upon themselves are almost overwhelming. Because psychic perception is a faculty of the mind, interpreted through the intellect, these inner messages found floating in the air can be as choppy as a kite on a windy day.

So, what are these so-called clairvoyants doing to undress our various costumed thoughts, usually purchased on a ready-to-wear rack labeled Past Sale Items? If you strip away the Hollywood aspect, you will likely be surprised to find that the majority of what they are "channeling" can be attributed to a keen understanding of people, coupled with an uncommon dose of common sense. This is not mental voodoo. They have simply mastered the art of reading people through the integration of body language and intuition.

By doing so—by becoming completely aware of a person on all levels—a fundamental shift occurs. For awareness is the source of seeing. The tone of voice, a look in the eyes, induces a special sensation. In essence, there is a conversation taking place before a word is spoken. Like an underground river, emotions, thoughts, and feelings flow forward, never ceasing to stream through us even if the mind consciously tries to stop them.

Let's say a self-proclaimed visionary confronts a woman with so many struggles written on her face that the lines resemble a map of Bosnia. She is dressed carelessly, her posture passive. She slumps and gazes downward, as if looking for signs of hell. Subsequent to being addressed, her expression remains vague, her eyes clouded. Her hand rests against her cheek while she absentmindedly massages the plain, gold wedding band on her ring finger.

The psychic says, "Boy, it looks like your life has been reeeeeeally hard. Times have been tough lately. You have concerns about your marriage and money." Suddenly, the woman springs out of her chair like a demented jack-in-the-box screaming, "Yes, yes! How could you possibly know?" Psychic phenomenon or an astute understanding of human behavior? Clearly, this is nothing more than the ability to tap into the range of emotions, however subtle, expressing themselves as symptoms before they have clearly registered in the person's mind. The information begins as conscious knowledge but eventually slips down into the subconscious mind. By simply paying attention, utilizing your full awareness, you can access and retrieve this information at will.

When you first meet someone, trusting your intuition is critical. I am by no means suggesting that you judge someone based upon preconceived prejudices. Quite the contrary. But, when you form a decision utilizing your intellect and emotions, you are only calculating two-thirds of the equation and expecting the correct answer. Your subconscious is capable of filing away thousands of observations that make up the entertaining music of mankind's performances. The slightest change in a tone of voice, the certain slip of the tongue, allow for a truer assessment of the person as a whole. Intuition is not the answer; it is the mode of transportation that will carry you straight to the deeper, inner place of all knowing we seldom visit. To suggest that this is where spirit, or God, or however else you wish to describe this higher power, resides is completely sanctioned by our souls. The throne on which it sits is no further than our own brains, as it swirls about amongst the chaos of our own thoughts. That's not to say it does not always require a journey. The journey for the search is essential and necessary. For without it, we cannot find our own truth. And the truth can do more than set you free—it can save your life.

Become intensely aware of your intuition. Learn to distinguish between it and indigestion, especially the type that causes diarrhea of the mouth. This disease takes the form of spewing off excessive excuses in order to protect ourselves psychologically. Instead of purposely putting aside our initial reaction, the first thought that pops into our heads, in favor of false justifications to manipulate a more fortuitous result to the meeting, why not examine the real reaction from the onset?

For example, let's say you're on a blind date with a man. Out of no fault of his own, he turns out to be short and balding, with a slightly crooked nose and a rapidly expanding Santa Claus belly. Not what you had in mind, right? You expected Brad Pitt. Okay, maybe not Brad Pitt but someone close to it. On the surface this man may seem hopelessly inadequate, so being the enlightened individual you are, you dig below your shallowness, only to discover that he is not only the wrong size and shape but also the wrong religion, the wrong nationality, the wrong . . . everything! Yet, something inside of you whispers softly that you might take another sip of this wine called infatuation. You drink again, further intoxicated by this inexplicable energy. No longer do you find it acceptable to walk away simply because this picture did not measure up to your frame. After all, what in the world could possibly hold the image together without one?

Logic plays no part in the intuitive process. Frankly, I'll go so far as to say that logic plays no part in anything. Like it or not, this is a participatory universe. Energy is constantly in motion, a changeless background against which all thoughts play a part in a continuous and endless story. Logic, however, operates in a strictly linear fashion. It cannot peek around a corner, and sometimes this is precisely where the mind must reach. Intuition allows us to do so. Is this simply guessing? No. Guessing is random; intuition is not. Likewise, intuition should not be confused with creativity. It is, as mentioned before, knowing something without the conscious use of reasoning. In that respect, intuition can and will enhance creative prospects, not control them.

Example: intuition guides the scientist to create the hypothesis, the detective searching for clues, and the doctor piecing together a particularly difficult diagnosis. Although the information materializes in an unorthodox manner, the answer will require vigorous verification. Deduct intuition from the equation and what you have left are intellect and emotion.

Conrad Hilton once said, "I know when I have a problem and have done all I can—thinking, figuring, planning—I keep listening in a sort of inside silence til something clicks and I feel a right answer." Albert Einstein is another prime example of someone who gave free rein to his intuition. While shaving, Einstein pondered the nature of time and envisioned a clock being hurdled through space, picking up speed and traveling faster and faster. That image led him to the development of the Theory of Relativity.

There are literally hundreds of examples of this nature. I recently read a true story, wherein a doctor stopped a patient from entering surgery because he felt something wasn't right with the patient's heart. Tests were undertaken, only to reveal that the patient indeed had a heart murmur, which would surely have killed him under anesthesia. When asked what gave him a clue, the doctor simply explained that he'd had a funny feeling. A hunch.

How many mothers can feel it when their child is hurt or in pain? When was the last time you made a statement with such conviction that when it actually occurred, even you questioned how you knew it would?

Intuition is holistic in nature. It does not burden you. Rather, it rises up in the mind, like perfume from the soul. The scent is sweet for it smells of the stars and the stones. It is from another realm, and once you enter it, your life will never be the same.

JUNG'S INTUITION

Swiss psychiatrist Carl Jung strongly believed that intuitive perception was a valued means for obtaining information. He eventually broke free from his mentor, Sigmund Freud, as Jung believed that mere self-observation and intellectual self-analysis alone were an insufficient means for establishing contact with the unconscious mind. Instead, Jung advocated a patient's use of intuitive awareness as a therapeutic tool toward establishing contact with our own hidden beliefs.

In the collected works of C.G. Jung, he describes the intuitive process as "neither one of sense-perception, nor of thinking, not yet a feeling, although language shows a regrettable lack of discrimination in this respect . . . intuition as I conceive it is one of the basic functions of the psyche, namely perception of the possibilities inherent in a situation."

HOW IS IT ACCESSED?

If you really want to expand your power to read a man's mind, the first thing you must learn to do is this: SHUT UP! Women have a particularly hard time doing this, especially when things aren't going their way. I am guilty of it myself. When I get upset, the first thing I do is get busy. If for some reason I can't find something to get busy about, I talk about getting busy. I talk a lot about all the things I am going to do, none of which I actually do because I am too busy talking about them. When there's no one left to talk to, which is inevitable, I talk to myself. Ah, but myself might have something sound to say and actually awaken me from my self-anesthetization. So, I compound the problem by drowning out the possibility of hearing any potential solutions with the aide of outside noise. Usually I listen to the news, which is guaranteed to depress even the most optimistic ostrich. Music is also an exceptional escape. Drums over here, keyboard over there, until suddenly I have a rock band playing inside my head. It is virtually impossible to concentrate on anything. Like my life.

But if you want to know what anyone is thinking, including yourself, it's imperative that you cultivate silence. We must quiet the mind as much as humanly possible. I am not talking about making your mind blank. The last time I cleared my mind completely, I had been knocked unconscious in a car accident. If I waited for my mind to draw the same type of blank again, I would be dead. There is no requirement for an empty mind, just a clear one. Stilling our minds completely would be as difficult a task as keeping a candle flame lit in the wind. Better to go inside and let the flame burn unencumbered by outside sources.

The most effective method for accomplishing this is meditation. Okay, so we've heard it all before, right? Perhaps, but I am not referring to the New Age guise this ancient art has undertaken over the years, where everything from special mats, clothing, and various other materialistic items have become a prerequisite to pre-meditation. With this Beverly Hills is Mecca, and you can just sort of feel its vibrations attitude, the very nature of the simplicity of the craft is lost. Probably somewhere in the mall. Albeit, the association between meditation and religion has dissipated, making it that much more mainstream and acceptable to the mere mortal, the idea that it is not an active but a receptive activity is still misplaced in the confusion.

Literally hundreds of books have been penned in the name of the art of "not doing." It is not my intent to challenge any or all of them. There are any number of important issues to consider when evaluating a specific form of meditation, all highly individual. Most importantly, did my old self change as a result of being meditated (not medicated)? If a certain method works for you, by all means do not desist. However you choose to penetrate the chaotic surface of the mind's activities, the allegorical absence of substance boils down to one main ingredient: a shift in perception by consciously redirecting your subconscious mind.

Researchers have determined that the brain is stimulated through focus and concentration, and by doing so, we employ more of the same. The mind's "job" expands by integrating the upper portion, the cortex, where we intellectually gather information, and the lower part of the brain, the limbic system, where we emotionally gather information. When these two worlds collide, an explosion occurs, out of which is created a world of independent existence wherein all possibilities exist. Thoughts no longer swirl around like leaves in the wind; they form a pattern of unmanifest promises, completely ignorant of the censoring mechanism we formed from our past mistakes and disappointments. Our spiritual stagnation is blown to smithereens. Our frame of reference no longer has edges; it literally spreads so wide and far we can no longer place boundaries on its borders. All without taking a single step toward a special type of clothing or sitting in a darkened room while assuming a cross-legged pretzel position, which I personally could never get into, let alone out of.

Through meditation, you transcend the limitations and lack that cause the majority of your problems. An inner, directional voice will not only show you the way but also how magnificent the journey can be. So, how does one differentiate between this mystical tour guide and our own mental mumblings and emotional drivel? First of all, your higher self is smarter than you are. If there is a God, and I truly believe there is, I finally realized that he's got it going on more than I ever will. My own intellectual vitality consisted of an ocean of ponderings, with negativity crashing in waves against a shore built with rocky speculation. Understanding and aligning to natural principles as old as the world itself does not involve confusion fraught with negativity. This is because it does not operate out of fear, which, in most cases, is nothing more than a negative wish. It does not instruct us through vindictiveness, anger, and pain. Instead, the messages from a higher source are equitable, even in a potentially dangerous situation.

Upon meeting someone, for instance, the small, inner voice inside informs you, quite politely, that something is wrong. "See this person, the real one you are talking to?" it says in a calm, composed manner. "This person is not good for me. He is a first class jerk, and the only person he'll ever love is himself. They have an energy level so low they are almost in hell, and they will take me there with them. High tail it out of here pronto, baby." The words are not mean-spirited; they are factual and to the point. (For the record, He doesn't sound like George Burns either.)

In fact, you may not hear a voice at all. As you begin to dissolve internal barriers to your self-realization, you recognize how you communicate with yourself, instinctively developing a deeper respect for the capacity to locate and retrieve necessary information through images, thoughts, and feelings. This is the screen through which we filter particles of particulars about people or about life for that matter. (This is discussed in detail further on in Speaking a Man's Language.)

While universal aspects apply to everyone, your own are unique. Should you take it personally? Hell, yeah. Your inner voice communicates with you in a specific manner. Learn how it looks, how it feels, how it "speaks" directly to you. This enables you to gain access to your inner voice at will, rather than by accident. Without realizing it, you will train your mind to see, hear, and feel information, allowing you entrance into the portal of human consciousness.

Next time you have an intuitive moment, analyze the motivation behind the action. When was the last time you called a friend, only to hear them explain that they were just thinking of you, that they were just about to give you a call, but you beat them to the cosmic punch so to speak? What ingredients so tastefully blended together to create such a delicious sign of serendipity? Next time you hear yourself say, "I knew I shouldn't have gone in the first place," or "I knew something bad was going to happen tonight," take a minute to explore the nooks and crannies hiding inside your decision. Uncertainty, mixed with a low self-image, are where most people's thoughts originate and lead to poor judgment and hasty decisions. Not a good recipe. By being in control, you allow your mind to work in its own way, without forcing it. Quickly and effortlessly.

Let's face it, when you bump into someone for the first time, it's highly unlikely that you'll be granted the opportunity to say, "Could you please wait right here while I meditate, maybe even talk to God about you, then I promise I'll get right back to you." By demystifying the process, meditation can be easy, almost exhilarating. And, again, quick. Anyone can meditate, anytime, anywhere. All it takes is a minute.

CHAPTER THREE

THE ONE-MINUTE MEDITATION

Minute. Meditate. Not two words you would normally see together. A shame, as one of the reasons so few people practice a daily meditation is because they are under the assumption that it takes time—and scarier still, effort. The grandiosity of self-appointed gurus we sometimes see on television and read about in magazines adds to the illusion of the enormous strain that must be involved in the process. What a load of crap! Meditation is a form of relaxation, originally designed to be both psychologically and physically comfortable. I have found that diving into the mind's depths is actually easier than ice-skating across the surface. The deeper you go, the more relaxed you are. It's not nearly as difficult as one may suspect (or been led to expect). In fact, whether you realize it or not, you practice this vertical trip through mind space on a daily basis. At least once, if not more. How? Nighty-night.

When we fall asleep, we automatically alter our state of consciousness within seconds. Brain researchers have determined that the mind emits four wave levels of consciousness as we pass in and out of sleep. Beta is the waking state of consciousness, where (hopefully) we are completely aware of our environment and experiences. When our body relaxes further, we drop down to an alpha state of consciousness. Here, we are still cognizant of our surroundings but not bothered by it. Delving deeper, our mind reaches the borders of sleep called the theta state. We dangle on the edge, much like a tear on the cliff of an eyelid. A sea of blankets envelops our mind and body

19

and although the environment may filter through, it will not penetrate the covers. Beyond this state, we reach delta, also known as dreamland. With a bit of luck, you are not in that state right now.

Ideally, your optimum state of awareness is the theta level, the most healthful state of consciousness, as your body and mind are completely relaxed. You can rewrite your resume, buy a new briefcase, and call a headhunter, but until you believe you deserve a better job, *on this level,* you won't get one. And, if you do, you won't keep it.

The majority of people don't realize how they created their circumstances. One day they wake up and feel completely powerless. "What am I doing, and why?" they ask, as they plod through their life unable to understand their actions. On a subconscious level, the answer is easy to explain. Based on past experiences, they created the present. Their thoughts programmed the subconscious to believe this is who and what they are.

Taking control means changing your subconscious. Otherwise, the faces change, the names change, but haven't you noticed that the same circumstances repeat themselves over and over again? Each situation, each relationship, simply picks up where the last one left off.

I will be the first to admit to being highly unqualified to dish out advice on relationships. Most of mine have been such rollercoaster rides that they would surely make the best of us vomit. What I learned, however, in a somewhat unconventional manner, is that my difficulty with the opposite sex was not facilitated by books about men from Mars and women from some other planet. (I did not need a Ph.D. to inform me that I come from some other planet.) This may work for some people, but I found it akin to reading a book about riding a bicycle. No material, audio or visual, can prepare you for either type of balancing act. Real change occurs on a subconscious level, with a deep belief that you deserve more. No one need show you what to do. You show yourself. And, you can do it all pretty much in your sleep. Or at least on that ledge before you fall off into blackness and an entirely boundless field of possibilities. This is the place where heaven touches earth and there are no secrets. Answers to questions appear, changes are automatically activated, and the announcement of the newly unformed no longer necessary.

Spiritualist Edgar Cayce referred to sleep as the "shadow" of death. His reasoning being that during sleep, our consciousness is unaware of our present physical conditions and enters into a larger awareness that transcends time and space; i.e., dreams. Cayce believed that we contacted our "sixth sense" here in the realm of unreality, which really created ours. Premonitions of future events and warnings of danger penetrated the blocks of time and space continuum with considerable ease. What I believe Cayce meant was that we become more aware, despite the fact that we are consciously less aware. During the early stages of the sleep process, the body is forced to shut down and the mind literally turns off. Sometimes you're not even quite asleep when this occurs. Needless to say, this is when the fun begins.

Before you throw this book in the trash with countless other New Age quick fixes, consider this: How many times have you seemingly dozed off at the back of a classroom, yet heard every word the teacher said? How many times has the same sensation swept over you while you were watching television? Have you ever "zoned out" in line at the grocery store? At your desk at work? In essence, you were meditating.

If falling asleep without falling asleep presents problems, try this:

Sit in an upright position. Balance your body's posture so that you are not swaying or rocking. Now close your eyes and take a deep breath. Concentrate entirely on your breathing, continuing to breathe slowly and deeply. In through the mouth, hold it to the count of five, and exhale. Repeat. Notice that your body becomes more and more relaxed with each exhalation. Observe your breathing, but at the same time, try not to control or interfere with it. Observing your breathing is one of the most ancient forms of meditation. With practice, you should find that during the exhalation, you will let go and become very relaxed, and during the inhalation, you will witness the mystery of inspiration. It is no accident that the word inspire is also defined as the intake of breath.

Now imagine a wave of relaxation entering both feet. It's moving up through each of your toes, up to your ankles, and through the calves, completely relaxing each muscle. Use this focus/relax method on every area of your body, all the way up to the hair on your head. Every freckle should be thoroughly relaxed.

BEWARE: Just as you enter a total state of bliss, what happens? WHAM! The voice of reason rears its ugly head. The ego mind vehemently disapproves of illogical ways of thinking, rationalizing the reasons why this cannot, and will not, work. The first maneuver will be to wander off the chosen path, straight into an ocean of self-pity and paranoia. After all, the enemy knows that your thoughts are what motivate you, and therefore, they can be easily ambushed—or at least drowned. Take your mind off of your objective and the ego becomes as unruly as a spoiled child throwing a tantrum in the middle of FAO Schwartz a week before Christmas. "Pay attention to me," it screams belligerently. "I am your material self, minus Madonna's money. We have more important things to think about, like shopping."

Your mind is doing a number on you. Don't believe me? When's the last time you set up an exercise routine, only to find that a week into it (if that), excuses appeared faster than hookers at a sales convention? It's just a small indiscretion at first, such as staying up too late the night before to satisfy some primal urge. Later, you come up with more substantial explanations for not rising at the crack of dawn to exercise. The boss wants you in the office early, or the kids need something from somewhere. They're all good excuses, right? Hah! Gotcha! The mind is not a willing participant and is eager to keep things exactly as they are, no matter how messed up that may be.

So, when your mind wanders off, give it a good slap. Harness your thoughts back to the present moment. Being in the right place at the right time is a direct result of our energy flowing smoothly. This can only happen if you are completely focused on the present, unattached to any end results.

If you have a different form of meditation, by all means use it. Remember, however, that just because it doesn't take a great deal of time and effort doesn't mean it's not working. Once you've reached a state of total physical and mental relaxation, provide yourself with a trigger. It can be as simple as placing your body in a particular position, joining your forefinger to your thumb, or saying a certain word in your mind. Make sure the trigger is something unique to you and that you keep it to yourself. Practice using your trigger for at least twenty-one consecutive days. This will ensure that the trigger is associated with a deep, meditative state.

Then when you need to relax, to completely clear your mind, all you have to do is take a deep breath and activate your awareness at will. Even if you do it faster than a guru at the Bombay Yoga Club, cultivating silence can and will bring you a deeper level of understanding, whether you want it to or not. Not unlike physical exercise, your mental musculature will increase naturally. Meditation is innately powerful. Five minutes a day is equivalent to one hour of sleep, and it can do more than change your perceptions—it can change your life. Seen through the light of faith, meditation can usher you into worlds unknown.

Guidance comes when you are still and quiet, hence the reason it's often referred to as the small, still voice inside of us. God can be realized through the truly intuitional perception received through meditation, but not by the restless mind. As the poet Rumi urged, "No more words. Hear only the voice within."

USING MEDITATION AS A CLEARING

It doesn't matter who you are, where you came from, or what socio-economical factors contributed to your background—if you are human and have problems, then odds are you started it. If the self we sprouted branched into flaws, it's not necessarily because we didn't build a sound structure. Perhaps it was because the foundation was rooted in the dirt of our past mistakes. In essence, we've been trying to reshape a form that has already been seeded. Our early childhood, our parents or caregivers, pruned us, shaped us. If you didn't get an A on that test, then you're just not that smart. If you didn't lose weight, no one would ever ask you out. If you don't get on the football team, you'll never go to college. And on, and on, and on . . .the tapes were endless. Preconceived ideas expanded across one track to the next. However, when they turned off the pre-recorded messages from the Sins of our Fathers, Volume II, so deafened were we by silence that we picked up right where they left off. Unfortunately, as psychologically damaging as these fear-based soliloquies may have been, they were nothing compared to the ones we have with ourselves. We turned up the volume a notch or two until we no longer heard the sweet sounds of our soul but rather a brainwashing mechanism, which suppressed our beliefs with such rationality that we accepted them as resolute. Our world remained intact, and we moved forward with a predetermined ceiling of our own worth that we neither willingly, nor consciously, constructed.

Sadly, a lack mentality manifests as more of the same. "If only I had a new job, a new man, more money (fill in the blank yourself), life would be wonderful." Sorry, karma doesn't work that way.

Your insecurities (a.k.a. your fears) convinced you there isn't enough; therefore, you should grab, chase, tackle, and basically strangle what you do have. All this accomplishes is the "blockage" of new energy.

Essentially, you mentally starve yourself. The universe is happy to oblige, after all, its job is to create more of what you believe. This is a law, which doesn't discriminate between sexes, races, or species. The President drops a book and it falls to the floor. You drop a book, and it drops to the floor. No exceptions.

This is why your intentions are so important. They are the roadmap to your destination, and hopefully, they don't resemble a Pocket Guide to Venezuela. In *The Peter Principle*, Laurence J. Peter concluded that, "If you don't know where you're going, you will probably end up somewhere else."

Let us nurture the free spirit, while continuing to feed the pragmatic mind. Your self-beliefs don't necessarily have to be negative in order to be destructive. *I've tried before, and it's never worked. Who am I to deserve love? Life is suffering, why should I be any different? What I want is too hard to get. I'm afraid I won't get it. I'm afraid I will get it.* These are all common complaints that perpetuate our limitations. But self-deception can take on a positive twist on these circuitous lanes, organically curving around bends the ego favors in its attempt to keep our minds caged in a city surrounded by prison bars. An Alcatraz for our souls

I want to win. I want to do it my way. I want to make the rules. I want to have power over myself and others. None of these false attitudes will make your life better, just more complicated, as by nature they cause anger, fear, and greed. You have allowed your ego to wrap you up in its own circle of hatred, a circle that never starts or ends but dances around endlessly, leaving you hopeless and weak. Recognizing this is all you need do to stop the carrousel and jump off.

Listen to yourself. The minute you hear a negative emotion lurking beneath your thoughts, erase the tape. Root them out and figure out why you remain so attached to this mask of misery. If you see yourself as fat, know you are thin. If you see yourself as unworthy, know that you are worthy. Refuse to buy into this preconditioned person you no longer wish to be. Remain aware and destroy the thoughts that held you back on a level where they cannot surface again. If you don't do this, you may still accomplish great things, but if you do this, you can accomplish anything. All it takes is faith and a lot of trust.

VISUALIZING THE MAN OF YOUR DREAMS

Life is full of choices. Most of us have a clear understanding of right and wrong, yet we continually get involved with toxic people, in toxic relationships—some potentially dangerous, if not deadly. You have the power to find happiness with satisfying, healthy relationships. Again, it's a choice you make and a belief that you deserve to have it.

Get comfortable and, using your trigger, completely relax. Now, give yourself permission to want whatever you want. This is not a joke. Think about it. So often, we don't even allow ourselves to want something. We've already dismissed it as something out of our reach, or out of the question, or impossible to begin with, so we stop trying. Consider this: it's okay to get what you want. This is not about setting goals and reaching outcomes. It's about feeling what you want.

Figure that out first. What do you want? Now, what do you *really* want? It may sound funny, but most of us stopped asking that question a long time ago. Somewhere along the line, what we wanted didn't really matter anymore. Someone beat it out of us and we just threw in the towel. It doesn't matter who did it, or how it happened, or where or when. We don't care anymore. What we care about now is understanding that nothing is out of reach. I repeat: what do *you* want? Now think about your relationships and the type of man you would like to compliment you and your life.

The answer may not come to you at first, at least not in the way you imagine. But keep at it. You will see pictures, have a peculiar sense, or sensation. Whatever it is, validate and support it. Each is a key to unlocking your own hidden desires. Think of the qualities that you desire in a man, physically as well as mentally.

Once you understand the kind of man you want to draw into your life, bring him to you. Close your eyes, go deep inside yourself, and summon the type of man you want to come to you now. Feel the energy of love coming to you and filling you up inside. Really feel it. Live it, breathe it. It is a part of you already. In other words, IT HAS ALREADY OCCURRED. Make a clear commitment to yourself that this is already so.

> "Some people actively retain illness and energy blockages, usually because it is more convenient or familiar to live this way." – Caitlin Matthews

CHAPTER FOUR

DEVELOPING YOUR FIVE SENSES TO CREATE SIX

A philosopher by the name of Gurdjieff coined the phrase the "sleeping man," a term he used to describe the average man. If the idea seems a bit far-fetched, the next time you are stuck in rush hour traffic, inching along like a drunken snail, take a good look at the guy in the car next to yours. Waking oneself up, according to Gurdjieff, required force of will. Otherwise, one was destined to plod along while sleepwalking and talking, completely unaware of one's unhappiness.

But one day this willful suspension of disbelief dissipates. The fog eventually must lift and the veils part, only to reveal an image of someone old and gray staring back at you from the mirror. *Who is that person? Surely that's not me? What happened? Where did the time go? It all happened so fast.* True. It did. That's because when you're asleep, time flies, and when you are wide awake, fully aware of your surroundings, living life to its fullest, time moves slower and with less effort.

If you assume that you will live to let's say eighty, and you sleep for approximately one-third of that, then only fifty some odd years are spent in an awakened state. Now, if you are only noticing about half of what you are doing, which means that you are not watching television while drinking a beer and eating junk food (or, worse, sitting around and daydreaming about doing those things), then you are really only alive for roughly twenty years.

To be fully awake requires one to be fully enlightened. Our senses must be ripened until they overflow with our subconscious juices. In other words, losing one's senses just may be the sanest condition possible. Unless this is the case, however, we rarely pay attention to what we are touching, tasting, or smelling, unless the culprit becomes bothersome or intrusive. There are literally millions of sensations sweeping over you in any given moment in time, and the idea of only five senses interpreting the data which creates our own personal vision of reality is absurd.

What we choose to see, or hear, is a subjective decision, not an objective fact. The human eye contains approximately 125 million rods (responsible for night vision), and 7 million cones (responsible for day vision) implanted upon the surface of the retina, the mechanics of which have been perfectly recreated in a robot. But can a robot duplicate the pleasure you feel when you see your husband holding his baby for the first time? Or the beauty of a sunset on a clear spring day? If our perception is infinitely flexible, serving the mind in any way the mind chooses, then the selection process becomes a mental activity, not physical. Billions of stimuli are excluded, or included, each as individual as a fingerprint. *I worked with that man once, how could he afford such an expensive car? She's getting flowers, again?* Are we visibly seeing the flowers, or are we reacting to the invisibility of our own preconceptions (in this case laced with jealously and fringed with envy).

This homogenous soup of the senses stirs up more than infrared wavelengths and electrical fields. The ingredients consist of a range—from the way the ground shutters beneath a person's feet when he walks to the hum of vibrations in his voice when he speaks of a new love. It is not merely observing the patterns the leaves on trees make but the pattern of the space in between. Often times, it is the break between the notes, which turns a particular piece of music into a masterpiece.

Aristotle and an entire ancient world agreed that it is our perception that confers reality. It is our flow of attention that transmits the power that lies dormant within the majority of mankind. The mind shouts out through the eyes, not just the mouth. And if you listen carefully, you will hear pain, or smell fear, or taste love. All of us are capable of detecting pheromones, the chemical our body emits if we are scared or sexually aroused. You can't see it, touch it, or taste it. You can feel it, although not physically. Yet, we all know it's there.

How many of us are even aware of where we are? Are you facing north or south? Are you above sea level or below? When was the last time you took a really good look at the street you work on? How many buildings surround you? What do they feel like? In other words, what feeling is being projected? Sound too metaphysical, too New Age? Come now, have you ever been in a room after two people had an argument? Anger creates energy often infused with adrenaline that can posses more power than gunpowder. You can *feel* it. What about when the air between people becomes so thick you can cut it with a knife? These are prime examples of the daily emotional pollution we unwillingly breathe.

What about the office in which you work? How many people work there? How do they feel? Are they bored, indifferent, angry, happy, or possibly psychotic? The next time you are at a party, make a mental note of the most impressive people there. How much of their façade is fashioned by clothes and the manner in which they walk, talk? Notice how people sit on buses, trains, and any other environment that restricts space. How do they react to being crowded in? Do they cross their legs, their feet, their arms? If you really, truly look around, you'll find direction.

If seeing places you on the right path, hearing helps you understand why. A direct correlation exists between hearing and comprehending—a synergy of inner sight and sound. Typically, the average person digests about forty-percent of what they hear. Instinctively, they block out background noise, the hum of appliances, street traffic, the voice of a boring teacher, their boss, their wife. Listening, truly listening, doesn't really require words. If you turn off the sound and watch the actions, you will witness a hemorrhaging of emotions.

In the past, I caused myself all kinds of untold personal pain. If the voices were soothing enough, or convincing enough, I didn't have to believe that they might be lying or deceitful. But turn off the sound, and you'll be amazed by what you find out about the greedy boss, the one who is always talking about how generous he is. Or the African American who speaks of how non-racist he is while passing over a white man for the promotion. Or what about the man who told you he'd leave his wife for you but took no action towards the goal? Take a good look at the couple that continuously reiterates how happily married they are. They are both leaning away from each other as they utter the words. Her jaw clenches. He continually glances down and hasn't made eye contact with her once while you've been there. Are they in love?

As for the rest of your senses, simply stay in touch. Volumes have been written about the healing power of aromatherapy. Olfactory awareness can allow you to concentrate, focus, and feel more sensual, or happy, or carefree. Smell a lemon and see if it doesn't uplift you. Inhale a good whiff of cinnamon and see if it doesn't increase your concentration.

Smell the food you eat; let it play on your nostrils and allow the flavor to seduce your tongue. Look at what you are eating. Notice its size, its shape, the texture, the feel. Listen to the room you are in. Is the sound soothing, loud, offensive? See the darkness of color, taste the saltiness of flavor, feel the roughness of texture.

Odds are you probably weren't aware of half the things going on around you. If you doubt me, next time you are home alone, blindfold yourself and see how far you get. Doing this requires you to become attentive and realize that all information in valuable. Even the most insignificant, mundane details can mean something. The big picture consists of small details. And the answer almost always lies in the seemingly insignificant. Do not allow yourself to become the chicken scolding the omelet.

Heighten the senses you already possess, become acutely aware, and open up to the infinite possibilities within the womb you once thought of as the unknown. Nestled here, you will find the inner child who possesses all the answers. No need to find the meaning, for the meaning will find you. Notice what you notice, and in so doing, you will naturally enliven your consciousness and employ the senses necessary to read right into people. Maybe you didn't understand why your boss constantly picks on you. If you pay particular attention, perhaps you'll notice that he picks on everyone. Or take the case of the secretary that won't give you the time of day. Observe, and you ascertain, and not by accident, that she's friendly towards other coworkers, thereby concluding that the situation is strictly personal. The conflict was likely sparked by a particular incident, which fired her up. You can then investigate and shed light upon a possible solution. By engaging your perceptions, you can marry each and all of your senses. Next time you are faced with an uncertainty, take a minute to remind yourself that you will assess the situation without boundaries, without limitations.

Reading people is quite similar to reading the weather. Although highly unpredictable, there are, for the most part, subtle signs in the air.

After awhile, the slightest shift in the wind will impact you. Isn't that where the expression, "It's in the air," came from? It's what makes a graveyard scary, a speaker inspirational, or a young woman fearful while walking through a deserted parking lot. You will automatically avoid becoming a victim of potentially life threatening situations because you are employing your full mental capacity. Insight naturally produces x-ray vision into what people do and say and, finally, what they are thinking.

Stay awake and pay attention. Hear a taste, touch a feeling, and see with your mind's eye. You must, for the world is a fierce place and because everything is at stake.

> As William Wadsworth grew older, he could no longer "see," yet he never forgot the light. In his poem, "Tintern Abbey," he describes his attunement with the world within, the perfect place of enlightenment:
>
> "...Until the breath of this corporeal frame
> And even the motion of our human blood
> Almost suspended, we are laid asleep
> In body, and become a living soul;
> While with an eye made quiet by the power
> Of harmony, and the deep power of joy,
> We see into the life of things."

PICTURING A PHOTOGRAPHIC MEMORY

Stop and look.

It's that simple. Never mind the fact that this is the same advice my mother gave me when I was five years old and I had to cross the street alone. With one exception: my mommy was one kick ass kid. She actually went so far as to disclose why. "You might miss something," she'd caution in that all knowing, all powerful voice that could scare buttercups into turning red. I swear I saw her do that once. And, of course, she was right. (I don't think I'll let her read this book.) But in this hurry up, microwave world, it's easier said than done, even when we're heading out into traffic, let alone the rush hours of our lives.

First of all, by stopping the picture so to speak, you literally freeze the image of someone in your mind. This can help you remain as cool as a popsicle in a heated situation. Take a deep breath through your nose and hold it for a minute. Now exhale through your mouth, letting go of any opinions, preconceptions, or prejudices you might harbor in that port of your brain. This is not about looking at anything or anyone out there; it is about reexamining your inner landscape from a clearer perspective.

Carlos Castaneda often recounted how his teacher, Don Juan, spoke of "stopping the mind" as the first step toward gaining the shaman's power. If your mind is speaking to you of its own needs and wants, then you cannot, and will not, truly observe and comprehend what's going on right under your nose. So, tell your mind to knock it off long enough for you to take a well-focused snapshot—to be developed at your own time and leisure.

Basically, what you are doing is improving your memory. Although I am sure they exist, I've never actually met a person with a photographic memory. The closest I've come is a character on a television series, conveniently solving some heinous crime by recalling a series of numbers longer than my arm. Are they strictly fictional? Surprisingly enough, they are not. They fall into a prodigious group of people known as "mental calculators."

One of the most famous cases happened to be a set of identical twins, who normally tested with IQs no higher than 60. Yet, Tweedledee and Tweedledum, as they became known (for their rather round appearance, thick glasses, and bobbing heads), could take a date any time in the past or future forty thousand years and almost instantly produce what day of the week it was, or would be. Considering that they lived in a mental bubble of their own, how could they possibly tell you, at the drop of a hat, what day Christmas would land on 25,500 years in the future? One of the theories was the possibility that they, and other human math machines, might be seeing the numbers. Rather than coming up with a calculation, they had memorized a certain formula or algorithm and could visualize the answer as quickly and precisely as a person could visualize their mother or father. In many cases, the person that cannot add two plus two but can recite the number pie to thousands of decimal places may be seeing it and reading it in much the same way that we would a computer printout. At one point, The Twins were asked how they could hold so much information in their minds—trillions of numbers, dates, and events. They simply said, "We see it."

The mistake the layman makes when trying to recall people and places is the inability to grasp the entire image rather than the minor details. If we stopped trying to fit the picture into a frame of an idea of what this person appears to be, we might actually come away with a truer, clearer portrait. By taking a mental snapshot, we cultivate the aptitude for remembering pictures at the speed of light, meaning the impression the light makes on our mind's eye. Later on, you can recollect that picture upon request, just as easily as a slide projected on a screen. The most miniscule detail, right down to a cat hair on a lapel, becomes excruciatingly apparent.

As with all things, practice makes perfect. Now I am not suggesting that you learn to recite pi to the nth degree, only that you concentrate on the intensity of each situation as it arises.

The ability to predict human behavior is not a second sight; it is a second look. Discovery is simply looking at something and seeing in it what someone else neglected to see. It already existed. Everything already does. Curiosity, observation, and focus are really all you need to discover the truth about anyone.

As William Blake once said, "the here and now mind of ordinary experience is potentially infinite, would we but pause to notice."

CHAPTER FIVE

TRUSTING YOUR INNER VOICE

Why is it that we don't react immediately to something that isn't right? Why do we wait until post humiliation sets in before taking action toward the injustice? You considered the strike an intentional affront in the first place. Right? Yet, angered, outraged, you did nothing. You were momentarily stunned into inaction—emotionally slapped so to speak. Later (ah yes, later) you came up with the perfect comeback, realizing what you should have said or done. In these situations, time passes much like a kidney stone.

When one processes this massive assault to the senses the curtain opens on the true drama. Life in reruns. The games of emotional hide and seek take center stage. The casual deceptions become background music. The jealousy lurking behind the smile. The lie behind the glint in the eye. The sudden burst of laughter disguising pain.

But why did it take so long to trust the initial response? After all, it probably hit you as a sick feeling in the pit of your stomach in the first place. Unlike hunches, which tend to be less immediate, gut reactions are most often physical, although not necessarily located in the abdomen or solar plexus. Who among us has not experienced a hair-raising experience, or a tingling sensation that slips down the spine like a poisonous snake, or a stab to the chest that is as cold and deadly as an ice pick? Our bodies naturally sounded an alarm. And chances are our trepidation was linked to something someone said or did. They silently projected their true intentions, unconscious of the impact of the exchange. Were you listening? Yes, just too late to react.

I used to be afraid to talk about my intuition, for fear people might label me as crazy. Even though I am (to some degree we all are), why add to the implication? And the truth be known, I'm not sure I believed in it myself. When I had a problem, I would ask for a sign—from a billboard, a book, a song lyric, something, anything. But then when I got it, and I always did (personally, I have been attacked by more books flying off of bookshelves than anyone I know), I would chalk it up to coincidence instead of synchronicity. Coincidence has no rhyme or reason, whereas synchronicity is an outward manifestation of our own subconscious mind. I ignored both explanations. Why? Because either way, they frightened me. There's a certain amount of fear attached to the non-rational self that makes me nervous.

The majority of us enter the world trusting our feelings, expressing ourselves honestly and openly, embracing the essential core of our being, the womb of our creative self. With raw, uncensored senses, we formulated our own ideas of tapping into a higher intelligence. Unfortunately, by the time we were old enough to understand, the conditioning began. We were told, repeatedly, that these "supernatural" sensations were a product of scary movies or an overdose of Snickers bars. Or, say you were scared of monsters in the closet, as I was, and could only sleep if the doors were completely closed, then these fears were likely dismissed with a cautionary warning about allowing our imaginations to run away from us. After all, monsters are not real.

Here's a thought: maybe, just maybe, these "monsters" were our own abstract fears. And they were real. We were afraid of the dark, of being left alone, whatever it may have been. It didn't really matter in the end if the monsters were real or not, now did it? As long as they didn't hurt us. "You're just being silly," our parents lamented. And so the first of many wrinkles creased our intuitive defenses.

From early on, in an effort to be accepted, we accommodated the belief structures of those around us, often at the expense of our own self-interest. In so doing, we denied our spontaneous impulses in a knee jerk reaction of logical thinking by following the crowd and not rebelling against authority. *Should I even feel this way? Should I tell them how I really feel?* The feelings we are told to suppress as children, remain so as adults. Your inner child may dance in ecstasy, but your outer adult will merely substitute a smile. One, at some point, we no longer find tenable.

The mind maker wielded such power in the world of society's standards that later on we questioned our own warning signs. Because the results may not be immediately perceivable, it's easier to shrug our shoulders and dismiss synchronicity as unsound. It's easier for the intellect to plunge into the part of the mind that judges and categorizes our experiences. It's easier to say, "Wow, that can't be right. I just made it up. Nah, that kind of stuff doesn't happen to me." Weeks go by, sometimes months, before your "feelings" are confirmed and you say, "Gee, I knew that would happen."

Come now, you probably weren't all that surprised when something unexpected happened. If you were just fired, didn't you sense it prior to the condemning course of events? Didn't you hear it in the secretary's voice when she informed you that the boss wanted to see you? Didn't you see it when he stepped back slightly and never sat down when you finally entered the room? Although the information may come in bits and pieces, a picture in the puzzle emerges. In short, your intuition works, whether you believe in it or not. That's what makes it so daunting.

Let's face it, to some degree, it's a control issue. If we don't believe in our intuition, and more importantly place our faith in the wonderment, then we cut the wires to our connection with a higher power that brings wisdom and knowledge. Randomness rules. But, by giving up our control, we actually gain the upper hand. We can no longer postpone risks or discount our insights. Instead, we are offered a momentary reprieve from chaos, and offered a surprise package, wrapped in God's blessings. It's the proverbial "aha," which comes at a moment of insight that opens up new possibilities.

It's almost as if once you commit to believing in your inner voice, then something magical happens. Instead of saying, I wish God would tell me what to do about this certain someone or certain situation, He will. God is synonymous with infinite intelligence, and His wisdom is inside of you. His spirit points this out at the most opportune moments. The signs are everywhere. You see a stranger and feel as if you've met him before. You look at the ocean and feel as if you are a small speck of an infinite being. Smelling a rose may bring about a burst of love. You dread a crisis, but when it comes, a wave of calm floats you through your worst nightmare.

By giving yourself permission, you will open up to a whole new world of symbols and pictures that come from way deep down inside of you, augmenting your own subconscious level of understanding. You will automatically tap into a reservoir of signals and signs. Do you remember your mother, or grandmother, singing you a soothing lullaby when you were a child? If you meet someone later on in life, and that same tune comes to mind, you can bet it's because this person makes you feel the same way you did then. Loved.

How many times have you said, "I shouldn't have done that?" Clearly, something told you not to do it in the first place. Failure to trust your intuition is failure to trust yourself. Do not dismiss that part of you that can't be categorized. Cultivate the habit of asking your inner self for guidance. Things will fall into place naturally; doors will open miraculously. How? Sometimes you will be given a miracle, sometimes you will just miss a train or a plane or pick up your child early from school on that particular day. If you live with spirit, you live with the beauty and the wonder of these surprises and the knowledge that anything can happen.

Carl Jung coined the term "synchronicity" to explain such "meaningful coincidences," and even though the word itself has taken on a life of its own, it really doesn't offer new explanations to the mystery itself. What outside of us could possibly organize time in such a way? All I can say is that there are no accidents. There are messages, rather like angels in training, but angels nonetheless.

When my mother explained death to me, she would always end with a consolatory, "It was their time to go." And now I finally understand what she meant. It's not a psychic ability that allows us to predict the outcomes of our lives, but rather us tuning into ourselves. The whole is merely communicating with the parts. As spirituality becomes more commonplace in our lives, the word itself will become outmoded, outdated. The necessity for an explanation of the occurrences of our lives will become as irrelevant as explaining childbirth. Understanding the patterns, and eventually predicting them, will become commonplace.

No amount of words can substitute for personal realization, the true inner voice. It will unfold and refold as arbitrarily as clothes in a dryer. However, one truth remains. We all want to live a comfortable, satisfying, unforced life. The way is easy. Listen to your heart and you will hear the answers. There's no better way to know others than to first know yourself.

> THE LANGUAGE OF INTUITION COMMUNICATES THROUGH FEELINGS: AN ANXIOUS FEELING, A NAGGING FEELING, A PERSISTENT FEELING, A GUT FEELING, A SUSPICIOUS FEELING, A DOUBTFUL FEELING, OR A HESITANT FEELING. BUT THE MOST IMPORTANT FEELING OF ALL IS A FEARFUL FEELING. DO NOT DENY IT. DO NOT IGNORE IT. IT CAN SAVE YOUR LIFE.

INTUITIVE INTELLIGENCE: MIND OVER MIND

I do not consider myself an expert in psychology. In fact, I dropped college courses on the subject because they didn't say anything new, and the old was the opposite of what I'd originally believed to be true in the first place. The paradigm persisted, and I learned that there is no mystery that cannot be solved inside your own heart or head. I sought, and could not find, classes in spiritual psychology, intuitive psychology, the psychology of nature. None existed in a reasonably definitive manner, or in the realm of serious, scholarly academia.

Rather than adhere to the linear image of reason, I chose to probe past it into a space that was more meaningful. A place just as natural to us as rationality, a place where thoughts have an invisible animating force, as capable of finding a lost loved one as it is to heal a terminal illness. A place that bridges the impassable gulf between mind and matter. The meaning itself slipped through the cracks of science, shunning things that could not be touched or seen. Yet nature itself supports that which cannot be seen or touched. How do birds know when to fly south for the winter? How do babies know to cry when they are hungry?

I would not even go so far as to say that I am particularly more prodigious at writing and researching, regardless of my years of experience. To be entitled with such an honor at anything would take a lifetime. Therefore, this shall be a rather short soliloquy. I am merely a student, constantly discovering the vast potential of our minds. However, to acquire this ability and use it for our own positive growth and benefit, rather than as a manipulative and controlling tool, one must look to a higher viewpoint.

To reference Eugen Herrigel's classic book, *Zen in the Art of Archery,* Herrigel states that the pupil allows the teacher to "bring into view something of which he has often heard, but whose reality is only beginning to be tangible on the basis of his own experience."

Zen in the Art of Archery is the story of a German who spends years learning the skill of Japanese archery under the guardianship of a strict Zen master. It not only deals with the physical aspect involved in this "sport," but also of the inner process required to achieve success: the state of effortlessness. As Herrigel explains, should the archer "deliberate and conceptualize, the original unconscious is lost."

In other words, you can only achieve success (in any area) by nurturing this "free-flowing inner momentum between your conscious and unconscious awareness." While attuned to the unconscious, yet remaining focused on the inner goal, one can step back from one's thoughts and turn them inside out and upside down by examining them from all angles. A master archer, Herrigel discovered, could intuitively distinguish his right shots from his failures before releasing the arrow.

What does any of this have to do with reading people? At some point, you will be able to distinguish the "right shot" of your true intuition from anxiety, confusion, or just plain old wishful thinking. Not unlike shooting a straight arrow, you cannot make it happen. You shift your point of focus, relax, and it comes to you. The synthesis of this infinite supply of knowledge, combined with the physical aspects forthcoming, is extremely powerful. Mind over mind.

PART TWO

THE POWER OF PATTERNS

"O, what men dare do! What men may do! What men daily do, not knowing what they do." – Shakespeare, *Much Ado About Nothing*.

CHAPTER SIX

LET'S GET PHYSICAL

With the publication of Julius Fast's book *Body Language* in 1970, Kinesics, the study of body language, hit pop culture with a big bang. Virtually everyone began analyzing the significance of crossed legs and crossed arms and, for the most part, came up with some pretty crossed signals. Fast himself warned that mastering body language could be a formidable proposition, given that the study itself is a mixture of *all* body movements, from the conscious to the unconscious—a potentially poisonous reality sandwich should one only ingest a person's physical appearance.

Then there remains the inherent problem of posers. And the question must arise: Does anyone know what enterprising type of weirdness is leaking out from the seams of the disguise? In other words, crossed legs, or parallel legs, can be a clue to what a person is feeling or thinking, or it could mean nothing at all. So, why bother analyzing the stained glass of a person's personality when what is truly needed is a two-way mirror?

Because no matter how unnecessary you find the need to decipher a person's physical attributes, illusionary or otherwise, how they walk the walk and talk the talk predominate our opinion of them. A study done at the University of California Los Angeles revealed that the impact of a person's performance was based mainly upon nonverbal communication (55%), while only 38% considered voice quality, and a mere 7% considered the actual choice of words.

Not surprisingly, prominent men such as President Johnson solicited lessons in body language when informed by his advisors that his arm movements appeared both "mechanical" and "predictable." Much to his chagrin, and ours, even after consulting with an expert he still appeared somewhat puppet-like during his speeches.

George McGovern practiced diligently with his voice, only to appear flat and uninspired.

On the other hand, Franklin D. Roosevelt mastered the art of movement so well that few of his constituents ever referred to him as handicapped. Rather, he radiated an air of self-confidence, never allowing himself to be seen in a compromising position—physically or emotionally.

Fiorello LaGuardia possessed such an outstanding knowledge of body language that he appeared to be "just one of the guys" in both Italian and English—and any other language.

George Wallace projected such an honest image that if you listened to him long enough you believed anything he said.

Let's not forget Richard Nixon, even though I have tried. Yes, Nixon, who openly admitted to using body language to manipulate his audience. Clearly, he was as inept at the art of movement as he was as a leader. His mannerisms were of a limited nature, further exasperated by exaggeration. The tone of voice, the gestures, the jerk of his head as if slapped when he heard something that personally affronted him, were indicative of a subsurface form of solace. No wonder he became a target for mimics and impersonators alike.

Anwar Sadat, a great political leader, wrote about his attempts to control his facial muscles as a child when Mussolini ruled Italy. In his most private moments, Sadat confessed to scrutinizing Mussolini's photographs, noting the intricate interplay of facial expressions, the varied poses of strength and aggression. Sadat openly recounted his fascination with his nemesis' abilility to conjure forth power and strength by the mere twist and turn of a fragmented feature. In an effort to imitate, Sadat stood before his mirror at home mimicking the commanding expressions. But, alas, it was said his results were sadly disappointing as he lacked the time or energy to debate the logic of the casual. He abandoned all hope, screaming imprecations in his own defense. Anwar Sadat admitted the truth. His face hurt.

Like any other good sporting event, observing politicians is best done on the big screen. Close-ups and rewinds make this medium optimal for studying body language. Next time a favorite candidate, or better yet your least favorite candidate, delivers a speech watch carefully. Observe the manner in which he leans forward (to appear more in touch with his audience). Pay attention to the expert way with which he uses eye contact, and the exaggerated use of gesticulating when speaking at length. Note the way he pounds the podium, points accusingly, and purposely pauses for applause.

In person, the typical politician shakes hands firmly and warmly, making eye contact and nodding frequently while listening to another's response. And what do they do more than anything else? They smile. And they smile. And they smile. They seek to be trusted, even if this means being deceitful. (Gasp, what's that you say?) For the most part, successful politicians are masters of not letting the whole truth and nothing but the truth be known. They have to be. They are well aware that policies will be modified, whether they agree or not. Scrutinize them and you will be less fooled.

Preachers also serve in a position in which overly exaggerated body motions multiply as quickly as dollars in their donation baskets. The majority of celebrated fundamentalists possess a frighteningly effective grasp of body language. Take Billy Graham, who has a haltingly clear conception of human psychology and its effect on an audience. Notice that he points upward when referring to heaven, a big smile on his face, his eyes sparkling brighter than a jewelry counter at Tiffany's. Hallelujah!

But wait, mention hell (yes, I said hell people!), and the finger descends downward, his face transforms into a mask of anger and fear. He shakes, yet still maintains an incredible amount of control over his words and movements. He tips over the wine cup of our emotions by becoming exactly what he is preaching, even if it's for a limited period of time. The audience is drawn in by his all-encompassing restraint. They look up when he says heaven and down when he says hell. These gestures, and others, are as tried and true as those of any politician.

What about the average mundane male? He's just as easy, if not easier to dissect. Most of us are a big ball of conflicting thoughts, values, and beliefs. But no matter how complex a person appears to be, patterns of behavior will emerge, quite unconsciously. They originate from the dark corners of a man's soul, which they seldom, if ever, visit. Tucked away in these cracks and crevices of their mind, lies the truth.

45

Start at the beginning. Hone in on a person's most striking traits. Within the first minute or two of meeting a man, you should be able to discern his approximate age, physical characteristics, vocal idiosyncrasies, and any telltale signs of suspicion. Add a few key questions, and you can successfully pinpoint such vital information as their marital status, occupation, education, and hobbies, depending on which subject you are most interested in.

The human body constantly disperses nonverbal signs of the condition of its inner self. Each experience we have may appear to be a minor shift in our perception, but this split second synchronization causes approximately six trillion chemical reactions to take place within our bodies. Biologically, fear, anger, joy, pain, guilt, suffering, and hatred, just to name a few, all originate in the mind, which in turn is processed by the brain and spewed out in the form of our voice, our facial expression, and our posture. The wiring connected to those emotions cannot be cut off, or simply rewired, without a great deal of effort and concentration. Essentially, the deceit would be as obvious as the truth.

Countless studies prove that when a person tries to mislead his emotions, his blood pressure automatically rises. The cranial nerves in the brain control both facial and vocal expressions, and delusional actions destroy one or the other. Or sometimes both. In other words, even if a person tries, one of the two will usually leak through. It could be as surreptitious as a slight film of perspiration on the forehead, a shift in the tone of voice, a micro-expression. The messages you receive may not necessarily be the ones they intended to convey because they are unaware of, or believe others are unaware of, the language with which they are truly communicating.

Our feelings are so inexorably connected to our behavior that many qualify as colloquialisms. How often have you used the following expressions: *I can't face it anymore; try to keep your chin up; keep a stiff upper lip; it made me grit my teeth; he bared his teeth;* or, *he shrugged the whole thing off?* These are but a smattering of phrases used to express an emotion.

Indeed, retracted shoulders often represent suppressed anger, raised shoulders most often relate to fear, and squared shoulders indicate excessive stress, and so on. The body's physical manifestations are directly linked to our emotional states. Is this not why a soldier stands straight and stiff? Is he not trying to appear mentally immovable? The cliché of a "ramrod up his back" definitely holds credibility.

What's even more interesting is that, over the years, our physical features freeze in the form of these often forgotten psychological emotions. Scared people have scared eyes. If a person is particularly mean, they generally develop an unusually thin upper lip and narrow eyes. If they spend the majority of their lives angry, you may notice that the ridge of the nose is pulled up and the gap between their eyebrows remains permanently furrowed. Belligerent, ill-tempered people also have an inclination to slump, an instinctual need to protect themselves. Pain and restriction often leave their personal blueprint of the person's life around their eyes.

Paul Ekman, Ph.D., author of "*Emotions Revealed,*" claims that "everyone has 43 facial muscles that work to express variations of the same seven emotions—enjoyment, surprise, anger, sadness, disgust, contempt, and fear." According to Ekman, you can play any man's game simply by reading their expression.

Further research into the science of face reading not only unveils what's on a person's mind, but the state of their health. Those who are under constant stress will have more lines around the eyes and forehead. People who are prone to stomach problems, especially stomach ulcers, will frown more often (think of the way a baby looks when he/she has gas).

Men who spend the majority of their lives womanizing often lean their upper bodies back, thrusting their pelvic area forward. As a result, they often roll their hipbones when they walk to make up for the excessive posture. People who are weak have a limited attention span, unable to focus on one subject for any length of time. Consequently, their eyes dart about like a drunken monkey. Conversely, if you meet a sage, a truly spiritual person, you will notice that they rarely look around. That's because they are powerful, strong, and well aware of where they are.

At last count, there were somewhere in the vicinity of 5,000 different languages (not including dialects) in the world today. It's no wonder that most countries rely upon a universal body language, which incorporates over a million different gestures. Signs a traffic officer makes in England will be equally understood in Peru. A music conductor uses the same movements in Egypt as in Ecuador. If a man wants to tell you he loves you without using words, I guarantee you would understand him no matter what language he speaks. After all, the language of love is still the most important language of all.

VOICES

The average person thinks at a rate of approximately 500 words per minute but speaks at about 125. With roughly 15,000 thoughts a day, we literally bombard our brains with billions of bits of data. Somewhere in the midst of this churning chaos, we must manage to organize the message we wish to deliver. Which words should we choose to keep? Which words should we choose to give away? And, more importantly, how should they be delivered?

Basically, two dialogues take place simultaneously. One involves the actual words, while the other involves the tone with which they are carried. Sometimes this horse and carriage combination does not necessarily fit together, leaving the listener to draw upon his own mode of transportation toward a suitable conclusion. How does the horse look? Is the horse fit, healthy? Is the carriage in good shape or wriggling about precariously on two wheels instead of four? Are there some screws loose?

Listen carefully, not to just the words but to the underlying message beneath the surface. Did they mean what they said? Did they say what they mean? After all, the soul sings or cries in the sound of a voice.

Think of your favorite disc jockey riding the airwaves at 6:00 AM. With a voice pumped full of confidence, he can jolt us right into the fast lane of life. At the end of the day, a similar wordsmith uses his mellifluous voice to melt away our daily stresses, literally lulling us into a mellow mood. How is it that they magically manage to manipulate our moods? In both cases, these conversational masters keep their voices even and low-pitched. No matter what subject they chose to challenge, the tone is aesthetically pleasing. Comfortable. If this is someone we can listen to, then this is someone we could conceivably talk to. Bottom line, we like them.

Verbal Vexations

If you drop the lower-pitched voice down a notch, the voice sounds forced and contrived. This tone often attaches itself to men who feel insecure (usually about their sexuality) and try to overcompensate by speaking in a more manly manner. Apparently, they associate an excessively lower tone of voice with strength and power, which, of course, is absurd.

Loud voices belong to pushy people, mistakenly weakening any possible opponent by simply shouting at them. Unfortunately, whatever they attempt to communicate usually falls upon deaf ears.

Those who speak too softly are not necessarily sensitive and sympathetic, but more likely, control freaks. By lowering the volume of their voice, they force people to strain to hear them or to ask them to repeat what they said—a power play to gain an upper hand over a situation. (Especially the case if they were previously speaking at a normal volume.) This is a common manipulation tool used by passive-aggressive types to produce the opposite of what they want others to believe. This could be part of a game—one they play because they are full of anger toward whatever psychological demon they haven't exorcised from their mind. Another possibility is that they are seeking attention. Speaking softly demands that one focus entirely on the person speaking. Exceptions are sadness, grief, or illness. Depressed people normally speak at a lower level. If they withdraw during the conversation, this is generally the case.

Not surprisingly, shaky voices belong to shaky people. It doesn't take a rocket scientist to figure out that, unless they have a medical condition, they are nervous and/or assuredly upset by someone (you) or something (you).

A harsh, gravelly tone, the kind that makes someone sound angry, usually belongs to someone that is. Brief bouts of anger erupt in a higher pitched voice, not one that remains brusque over an extended period of time. This person has issues. Not only are they mad but they will take it out on the first person they find. Men with this type of voice are often viewed as bullies.

Dotting every *i* and crossing every *t* is really annoying. The person comes across as extremely rigid, and righteously so. These folks believe they know more than you, and no matter what you say, they'd be right. Worse, they tend to be oblivious to their condescending manner. Try explaining and they bark back, which, unfortunately, is worse than the bite.

I have been told that whiners are not necessarily complainers. Hah! Even if they aren't, they are perceived as such. Think of *The Nanny* and Fran Drescher. She sounded unsatisfied, even when she held up a new pair of Pradas. By moaning and groaning, the whiner demonstrates how strongly they feel about a subject—and that they will continue moaning and groaning, and whining, until they get what they want. Whether it's downplayed or not, it's still a way of manipulating someone without appearing to do so. As my mother would say, "Quit whining!"

People who mumble can be equally as annoying. For the most part, they have something to say but fear no one wants to hear it. Either they are self-conscious about the subject matter, or they lack the confidence to say what is really on their mind. The possibility also exists that they can't articulate the message they want to get across. They often mumble a courteous greeting, following it up with a weak handshake. They appear sad. Then again, a lot of people mumble when they get tired or sick. However, if the person appears to have low self-esteem, count on the former rather than the latter.

Speaking of the former, another tone fitting a similar profile is the dull and lifeless voice. These types have lost touch with who they are and therefore cannot help but keep an emotional vocal distance from other people. Unlike the staccato, choppy tone, the lifeless tone may contain more than a fraction of fear. If you know that the person does not normally speak in this manner, then rest assured that something is wrong. At first, you may become more animated in order to compensate for their lack of reaction, then you'll get frustrated, possibly even angry, when you realize that this isn't helping. There's almost a kind of resentment you feel when the other person won't respond to you. You can't get through and finally give up trying when you realize they've sucked the energy right out of you from trying. Because they are not communicating effectively, they quite often appear to be dishonest. Don't put it past them.

The sweeter than honey voice can be particularly dangerous. Look closer and you will find a razor blade buried inside this candy bar. Be forewarned. Likewise with the breathy, Marilyn Monroe type of voice. Anna Nicole Smith tried it and look what happened to her. In real life, it comes across as insincere. Save it for the bedroom, and then ooh-la-la yourself to death.

Those that have an attacking tone, especially when it's not warranted, are just looking for another way to beat you up. Run.

Do you know someone that says the first thing that comes to their mind? There's no conception of editing the words before they spill out of their mouth. Usually they are unaware of what they are saying and remain ignorant to the fact that they may have hurt someone's feelings. Complete disregard for political correctness is dubious, not to mention dangerous. Prejudice frequently lies beneath the darkened waters of brazen comments. Diarrhea mouth is a sickness.

Barring a mentally challenged person, a limited vocabulary belongs to someone with limited awareness. I am not referring to a person who lacks fancy ten dollar words, which make them sound like a walking encyclopedia. Quite the contrary. I am talking about a decent knowledge of what means what. Someone who believes an impotent man has reached a position of status in the world has a problem.

Those who constantly put you down usually don't feel good about themselves, so they try to make up for it by making you look bad, too. If this behavior occurs in front of other people, particularly if they know you both, then the person is jealous and feels threatened by you. Insecure people often build themselves up by tearing others down. The same holds true in the case of those who constantly contradict you. They are taking the opposite position of yours on purpose, usually in the hopes of undermining your credibility.

Ever meet someone that just talks and talks and talks, even if no one is listening? So entranced are they by their own voice that even if you spoke they probably wouldn't hear you—or care about what you said even if they did. They are quite commonly social misfits who chat away to comfort or console themselves. Silence would force them to deal with their own issues, which they have been trying to avoid at all costs. They'd rather interject something silly than be uncomfortable. Nod, smile, and be pleasant. The minute there's a chance to get a word or two in edgewise, say something like, "Gotta go."

I used to have a friend that complained constantly. He gave new meaning to the word entitlement. Why? I don't know. I don't want to know. This verbal victim craves attention, thereby seeking yours. But, here's the thing. No matter what you say, they will find some excuse for it not to work. They are the kings and queens of the "yeah, buts." They'd rather complain, because if they solve the problem what would their life be? They have fallen in love with the problem. If you're stuck with this type, turn on the television, file your nails, and let them keep talking. Anything you have to add won't do any good anyway.

Psst, come here . . . I want to tell you a little secret about gossips. People who gossip all the time are out of control power mongers. If they talk about what everyone else is doing wrong, they can only be right. You may think that busybodies are interested in your life because there's not a whole lot going on in theirs, but that's not necessarily the case. Here's the other possibility: they're trying to get the scoop on what you are doing so they can keep one step ahead of you. They are often sneaky and two-faced, appearing to be your friend in the hopes of extracting information. These are the kind of people who will get into a deep conversation with you at work, only to finally ask how much money you make. They throw you so off guard that chances are you will tell them. Jealously is frequently a motive. Watch out. As Sigmund Freud once said, "Envy seeks to destroy."

"You know, I was going to say, but couldn't quite remember, but, honestly, how do you feel about that?" Meet the quintessential yes man. Those that can't get to the point are covering up internal insecurities. Afraid of being wrong and/or making waves keeps them from taking a stand at all. What they are doing is waiting for you to make a decision, so they can then agree with you. Let's say you're not willing to voice your opinion and instead ask how they feel. It's hard for them to make up their minds because they don't have one. They are borrowing yours. In their eyes, one brain is better than two.

Another type of person forcefully trying to get in your good graces is someone that tells you way more than you need to know. In their desire to bond, to get you to like them, they share intimate details, crossing boundaries right into the, "Too much information, and I don't want to know," category. Getting too close too quickly will alienate anyone. The only people that like this type are the ones that do it themselves. Like attracts like.

When people preface what they say with an apology, such as "I'm sorry, but can you tell me where the men's room is?" followed by a pathetic, please, they usually aren't sorry at all. What they are trying to do is appear polite, and not doing a very good job of it, either. Could be they are shy, or perhaps suffer from low-esteem, but whatever the reason, they don't like to call attention to themselves. They will use few words and try not to speak up unless absolutely necessary—anything else would mean they are a burden to you, which may well kill them.

Do you know a snore bore? They put you to sleep with their voices, whether you like it or not. They drone on endlessly in a repressed, monotone

tone of voice. For one thing, they are not trying to be your best friend, even if you think they are. The disinterest is intended to keep people at arm's length, as that is the only way they can stay on top of the game. If you can't get close, you can't find them out. If it's not typical behavior, it could be they are simply angry at something or someone, and you should investigate further. Also, a flat, unemotional voice can be a tip off for anger and resentment. If you tell a friend you just got a raise and they respond with a dry, "That's nice," be on alert. They are most likely jealous and resentful. If this is not the case, go back to sleep. You're better off. You'll never receive the type of feedback you require, and you'll only deplete a lot of energy trying.

People who are too blunt are bullies. I'm talking about brutally honest, to the point where their only desire is to intimidate you. Their lack of diplomacy is indicative of a lack of maturity. Don't even try to engage in combat. You'll only be entering the world of a six-year-old brain.

Now on the opposite end of the spectrum are those that will flatter you, flatter you, and flatter you. In the beginning, it might be nice—I mean, who doesn't like to be admired? But when it crosses the line into excessive, one must remember the line by Confucius: "Never trust a person who is fawning." This is usually an opportunist, and once they get what they want from you, they will drop you like a hot potato. Watch your gorgeous self.

Let's not let the old slip of the tongue slide by. Freud first coined the colloquialism in his 1901 book, *The Psychopathology of Everyday Life*. He said, "Something one did not wish to say: it becomes a mode of self-betrayal." A man can unintentionally betray himself by forgetting crucial information and accidentally replacing it with something they really meant. Like calling a woman by another woman's name. Or saying something like, "I wanted to mate her," instead of, "I wanted to meet her." Freud demonstrated how the actions of our everyday being, such as slips of the tongue, forgetting familiar names, and mistakes in reading and writing, were not accidents by any means, but uncovered significant clues toward interpreting our personal problems. This could come in very handy indeed.

Think that self-criticizing people really don't like themselves? You can bank on it, baby. If someone says they'd forget their head if it wasn't screwed onto their body once, then it's nothing to be concerned about. A dozen times? Perhaps you should help them look for it in a duffel bag. Their motives for repeatedly putting themselves down can be quite complex, but for the most part they are trying to accomplish one of two things. They are either hoping you will agree with them, thereby giving them the much-needed encouragement and the ego boost they desperately seek. Or, they are hoping you disagree with them, giving them encouragement and the ego boost they desperately seek. Basically, if they bring their faults to the forefront, you won't have a chance to. In a strange way, what they are really trying to do is reach out to you. Approve, or disapprove, it doesn't really matter.

Humorists who use jokes as a form of criticizing themselves, or others, are a bit more complicated, especially if the sly remarks rest about a centimeter on the vulnerable side of sarcasm. To say they are clowns is beyond a cliché... After all, we can all poke fun at the expense of others. Comedy diva, Kathy Griffin, makes a successful living with her wildly hilarious observations of the rich and pseudo rich. It's a funny joke, made funnier by the fact that there's a modicum of truth to the cutting remarks. Likewise, those that use this technique on friends and family intend to hurt and humiliate, without appearing to do so. For instance, one makes a critical remark such as, "You've put on a bit of weight, any more and you'll be in line for a job with Shamu," then follows up with a, "Just kidding," chances are, they weren't kidding. If the humor is self-directed, it can be a form of self-protection. Either way, it's a way to mask their true objective, and maintain a distance.

Look, damn it, anyone who purposely perpetuates anger is mad. Trust me. They are mad and miserable. Worse, they seek company. Run. Hide. They thrive on pissing you off. In fact, they've probably saved up things that they know will push your buttons. Furthermore, they do this all under the pretense of giving you advice. For instance, if you have just met a new man and things seem to be going well, and then he leaves for a trip, these people will stick their nose in and remind you how easy it is to "pick someone up" when you're staying at a hotel. And, of course, he'll visit a strip bar. Before you know it, you'll be so paranoid about him leaving you'll forget to be happy for him. Stay away from troublemakers. If they're that desperate for entertainment, suggest they meddle in someone else's life.

Pardonez moi, a word about people who use their foreign tongue in front of people who only speak English. Not only does it make other people feel uncomfortable, because they don't have a clue what you're saying, it automatically alienates them. If that's their motivation, move on. The only time it's excusable is if they sincerely have trouble speaking English. Otherwise, it's just plain rude.

I used to take my daughter to a pre-school owned and operated predominantly by Indians. The women there often spoke to each other in their native tongue. One day I dropped my daughter off and checked her in with the usual morning flurry of sign and run. I had an important meeting that morning, and they saw me fully made up for the first time. Anyway, I'd gotten a little, teeny bit carried away, and I'm sure I appeared a bit overdone for 7:00 AM. One of the ladies commented to the other in their own language about my appearance. The thing is, my parents spoke the same language, and although I never really learned to converse in it well, I understood every single insulting word. I listened for a minute, then just as I walked out the door, I turned and said (in English), "Thank you for pointing out that my lipstick is too bright and makes me look like a demented clown. I'll be sure and fix it right away. Have a nice day." The ladies' jaws hit the floor faster than a broken elevator.

Speaking of my daughter, I also have a tendency to nag her a bit. My excuse is that I love her, so I want to make sure she does what's best. Frankly, I know I bug the crap out of her, but in a funny way she likes it because it does make her get the job done (especially homework). Now, if you're nagging an adult, it's a different story. Nagging translates to controlling. It is also one of the main reasons couples fight. You don't need to nag an adult.

Those who swear a lot do so for the effect, especially if they are around people who don't use profanity as part of their everyday vernacular. Let's face it, they will call a lot of attention to themselves if they take this approach (especially women, as most men are disoriented by a woman that uses excessive profanity). Thus, they have a certain amount of control, not unlike a bully. If you're up for the test, throw it right back in their face, otherwise they won't back down. If you get angry, they have caused a reaction and therefore gained power. Upon occasion, the person may be trying to keep someone at bay, but it's more likely that if they're not doing it for the shock effect, they are simply trying to be cool.

What about people that talk the talk, but don't walk the walk? All of us know someone who will promise the moon, and then you don't see or hear from them until many have come and gone. In most instances, you need not figure out these people, as they are simply not worth it. Good riddance to bad rubbish, as my mommy used to say. (I mention her a lot because, as it turned out, she's smarter than I thought.) However, there are times when someone reliable completely flakes on you. If they say they will do it and stall, it's because deep down inside they really don't want to. What they are avoiding can be extremely revealing. Putting up with the stress of doing something is much easier than not doing it—unless it's unpleasant, uncomfortable, or offensive to them. Make sure there isn't an explanation or some sort of internal struggle.

The man of few words may be mysterious to some, but frankly, he scares me. These "just the facts, ma'am" types rarely offer more than a direct answer to a direct question. Getting anything else out of them, such as an opinion, can be a bit like pulling teeth. This may make them seem quite meek, but chances are they not. There could be a host of reasons why they only speak when addressed, or worse, talk only when they want to talk, but one of the most common is a passive-aggressive approach to dominating the conversation. Another possibility is that they are simply self-absorbed and self-conscious. This is their way of shutting themselves off from the world. They don't want to try anything new or meet anyone new, which would only disappoint or hurt them. There are some definite psychological problems brewing beneath the surface, and if you're not careful, one day they will find it so hard to keep all those feelings pent up that they will explode like a volcano. After that, they'll go back to their short, often generic sort of responses like *I guess,* or *who knows,* so they can feel even more unaccepted by you and the rest of the world.

Last but not least, I must articulate upon one more verbal variation, which I feel is nothing to joke about. The laugh. The debate about whether or not a laugh fits into this category or not has never been established. Whatever. I say it's verbal because I have yet to see how it is related to strictly an expression such as grins, and smiles, and other pleasantries. So, whether it be a girlish giggle, a mild chuckle, or a deep belly laugh that brings tears to your eyes is not the question. Laughing is always acceptable, as long as you are laughing with someone and never at them. Otherwise, as they say, laugh and the world laughs with you.

The single most annoying voice? People who talk too fast. This puts off more people than any other form of speaking. Why? Because this speed freak spins a yarn so quickly it will literally make you dizzy. There are countless reasons why Mr. Type A goes off on a tangent. One is that they are lying. Another is that they simply aren't secure enough in what they have to say so they figure if they spit the words out quickly enough, you won't really hear them. Another is that they come from a large family. Those that did learned to say what they could, as quickly as they could, and the habit stuck with them. It could also be a sign of nervousness, impatience, or drug use. You'll have to get them to slow down to figure out which.

Actually, too much of anything corrupts the communication. Speaking too slowly can be equally as annoying, especially when the vowels are drawn out like string cheese on a pizza. Too loud can be deafening, too monotonous can be boring, and too high-pitched, just plain old distressing.

A pleasant voice is flowing and modulated, the words spaced nicely by drawing out vowels and enunciating clearly. The jaw is open and relaxed, which avoids being too high-pitched, too low-pitched, or too nasally. The volume is tuned to the medium level.

What's the most attractive voice? One that shows enthusiasm. A happy, upbeat, positive person instills confidence. As stated, just don't go overboard. Even too much pep can cause one to puke.

> Use your abdominal muscles to control your voice. Holding the stomach in while speaking enables you to allow the right amount of air to exit with the words, thereby allowing you to control tone and volume. Take a deep breath, relax, and . . . speak from your heart. You can't go wrong!

FACIAL EXPRESSIONS

According to researchers, approximately fifty-five percent of a person's communication is formed with the face. That's a pretty impressive feature. Or should I say features? Phonetically so. Seems that if the words dripping out of your mouth are not harmonious with your facial expressions, they become mute. In more ways than one. Doesn't matter how eloquent, persuasive, or faux Faulknerian they might trifle to be, words in and of themselves mean nothing. It's the essence behind them. In other words, the word hot cannot force you to break out in a sweat. Speak, and no one gives a darn unless you act like you mean it.

Examples abound. How many times have you heard someone say, "Sure, everything is just fine," and you know damned well that it's not true? All you have to do is look into their eyes and you know. I've watched countless numbers of celebrity couples stand side by side and tell the world just how happy they are together, that their relationship couldn't be better. Yet, when you look a bit closer, you will notice that they aren't standing together, that they aren't looking at each other for that matter. In fact, one of them is often looking down, the jaw tightened, the lips pursed, and the chin jutting forward. If the eyes and the face suddenly come down, it's usually a sign of guilt. Needless to say, this couple filed for divorce two months later.

The face expresses the most powerful non-verbal communication within our possession. In fact, we count on it when words would be inappropriate. If someone says something completely out of place, a smile can indicate that it doesn't matter, that it's clearly understood that the person missed the mark. A smile can also indicate that we are happy to see someone, whereas if we weren't we would have a tendency to keep our mouths and lips straight, or even frown. A downcast look can let someone know immediately that you are unhappy. At a rock concert, you can merely lift an eyebrow or twist your mouth and instantly convey a message of conviviality. And, if you are still not convinced, then remember this about your mother: THE LOOK. Remember, THE LOOK? When I got that look, man oh man, I knew I was in big trouble.

It worked so well that I use it all the time. My daughter instantly understands where I am coming from and (usually) won't mess with me. Yes, she knows me well, and unfortunately, she has seen the expression one time too many, I am sure, but I've used that same expression on her friends and received the same reaction. Even a dog can sense your feelings by the expression you are wearing when you bark out a command. My dog is a genius, of course; however, as is the case with infants, animals just know.

So, maybe you think you can hide what you're thinking? Perhaps you can. But even if it's for one brief millisecond, your face will always give you away. Most people won't see it, but it's there. Pay attention next time someone says they are happy to run an errand or help out in a certain situation. They may say they are fine with it, but watch their expression. A quick wrinkling of the nose in a flash of disgust may be detected at the end of the sentence. It's called micro-momentary facial expressions, for obvious reasons.

Over two hundred years ago, Charles de L'Epee, a French priest, invented what is now known as sign language. After observing two deaf sisters using their hands and fingers to communicate, he developed the rest. Part of what he taught, however, was the use of exaggerated body gestures while signing. For instance, you show a question by having a questioning look on your face. You'd have to be blind not to see the benefits of two methods in which to get the message across.

WHERE DO OUR EXPRESSIONS COME FROM?

Scientist Charles Darwin studied the faces his baby son made in his crib and compared them to apes. Although they were not identical, he found many similarities. For instance, his son grinned to show happiness, while the ape was demonstrating fear. After years of study, Darwin decided humans evolved from apes, and so did our expressions. This is one of the ways in which he coined the phrase the "muscle of difficulty" when the brows are pulled down and together.

Keep an Eye on Me

Our eyes are the most expressive feature on our entire body. It is said that they are the mirrors to our soul, and I can't argue. We even use our eyes when communicating with complete strangers. When caught in a narrow pathway with oncoming pedestrians, how do we signal the right of way? We make eye contact, and then look in the direction we intend to pass. Sometimes this doesn't always work, and we end up doing a little dance. No words are exchanged. They are unnecessary. Who has not experienced "a look that could kill," or an "I'm available" glance?

Ah, this leads us to love. Specifically, love at first sight. Cupid on speed, or at least a good old-fashioned caffeine high. Is there such a thing as love at first sight? I believe there is, and trust the eyes to tell you first. If someone is truly smitten, their pupils will enlarge. There will be a slight crinkle around their eyes. They will generally look at you for approximately four seconds, two to three seconds longer than a normal gaze. They will glance at you more often and literally catch your eye as much as possible. Michael Argyle in his book, *The Psychology of Interpersonal Behavior,* noted that during a conversation, people look at each other thirty to sixty percent of the time. If the amount of time were to exceed sixty percent, according to Argyle, it indicated that the person was interested—and not in what they are saying.

Try it. Next time you see a stranger, hold their gaze a fraction longer than typical and see what transpires. You may be shocked to find yourself speaking to him within seconds. And you may even find yourself liking it.

Similarly, if someone doesn't like you, their eyes give them away. Picture Mohammed Ali in the ring just before a fight. He literally locks eyes with his opponent, then narrows them, continuing to penetrate deeper with an unflinching stare. At once, he intimidates, dominates, and threatens his adversary, all with his eyes. On rare occasion, Ali's nemesis would raise his eyebrows and fix their eyes open, in a look of astonishment. They lost.

There would be no need to speculate upon the inappropriate use of sunglasses. Obviously, the person has a need to hide. Was anyone shocked to see Jack Nicholson wearing sunglasses to the Academy Awards? Or anywhere else for that matter. Why? Well, who knows with a creative person such as him? But the name of the book is *How to Read Any Man's Mind* and, although he may not be any man, I can venture to guess his ulterior motives. The person wearing the glasses feels protected and is under the impression that he can stare without being noticed. This is generally not true, for if someone continuously dons dark glasses, the other person may freely conclude that he is staring all the time.

Prescription glasses are an exception to this rule. However, they can still convey a negative connotation. If someone removes their regular glasses while speaking with you, especially if they look away simultaneously, they not only refuse to see you anymore, they also don't want to listen to anything you have to say. If they continue to look away once you've stop talking and they start, then it could be an indication that they are lying to you or feeling guilty about the subject matter altogether.

If you notice that someone has a chronic eye twitch, you may want to check on what's really going on in their lives. When we are acting against our true selves, our body will find a way to tell us something is wrong. An eye twitch is a muscle contraction, most commonly brought on by stress. Almost without fail, once the problem is eliminated, so is the twitch.

Excessive blinking can also be caused by stress (the same type of stress as a twitch). Usually people who blink a lot are not the most forthcoming. Unless they relax the muscles in their face, and fix you with a firm gaze, they are not being honest with you. If pushed, they will look away, as if they have something to hide. Take heed. If they are trying to ignore you altogether, they may close their eyes for a bit longer than normal or cast their eyes downward—a sure sign that they are upset, shy, or hiding something.

How do you tell if someone really doesn't have a problem in any of these cases but is just feeling down and sad? Take a look at their eyebrows. If they are drawn together, it doesn't matter what their eyes are doing. It's hard to draw your eyebrows together unless you are genuinely depressed.

Do not stare. Staring is reserved for non-persons, inanimate objects, animals, etc. Staring is impolite, a way in which a social snob treats one they wish to cut down to size. Or they may do the opposite and give them a slightly unfocused look (usually reserved for waiters, or servants in their home, and the likes—or in this case, the dislikes). These pseudo-snobs take the same position when faced with an abnormality, or handicap, which they can't quite bring themselves to acknowledge. Confident people are sensitive and try to see everyone eye to eye.

On Being Nosy

The nose can smell trouble a mile away. When telling a lie, white or any other color, a person will touch their nose with greater frequency. If they are talking while they do so, it's because even they think that what they have to say stinks. If you are talking, then they think that what you have to say stinks. Either way, it's pretty fishy. Also, if someone has their nose in the air, it's a pretty good indication that they are looking down at you.

One thing that must be mentioned about the human honker is that it is the most stress-sensitive point on the body. Just punch someone in the nose and you'll see what I mean. All kidding aside (although if your fist hits below the nostrils and jams upward, you can render a man more helpless than if you hit his second most stress-sensitive spot), the nose knows. Don't ignore it.

Smile, You're on Uncanny Camera

According to experts, something in the order of fifty different kinds of smiles exist in the world today. I don't know how they know this. I don't care. My baby had at least a couple of hundred, so I'm not going to buy into that. I mean there's a polite smile, a deliberate smile, a Charlie Chaplin smile, a compliance smile, a listener smile, etc. I could go on and on. But why? Most of these you can figure out yourself, so I won't bother talking you down like so many books I can't stand. There's really only one that matters the most and a few others worth mentioning.

First and foremost, we have the genuine smile. So, how do you determine if the smile you are receiving is authentic or not? The corners of the mouth curve up, the lips part slightly with the teeth showing, the cheeks are raised, and there is a crinkling around the corner of the eyes. You can take away any of these eye opening factors, except the latter, and still have a smile. A smile, a genuine smile, comes from the eyes. It lets people know immediately that you are friendly, approachable, and that you like them. It allows them to relax and open up to you. That's pretty powerful stuff.

If the lips remain closed and the mouth is pulled back, it generally signifies happiness. People will most often display this smile for those that they are most comfortable with. Watch someone's face when they read something they find funny. This is the smile they will most often use.

A broader smile, with the upper teeth showing and the mouth slightly open is the most common smile and denotes that a person is genuinely glad to see you. Smiling with the lips in is usually an indication that the person is feeling shy and a bit out of place.

A big fat grin, accompanied by dull eyes, will never convince anyone that it's an authentic gesture. Neither will tight or thinning lips. It gives the appearance that you're not telling the whole story. If saying, "Don't worry about it" follows this expression or "It's not a big deal," they probably don't mean it.

Biting the bottom lip is most often associated with repressed anger or hostility. They are trying their best to control this gnawing feeling; nevertheless, it manifested itself by chewing upon the one thing they use when they speak. If they shake their head while continuing to bite their bottom lip, they are most likely mad.

Because people generally get a dry mouth when they are nervous or anxious, they will lick their lips to compensate. Either that or they drink alcohol and/or smoke. This can also be a sign of attraction. A sort of, I can't wait until our lips meet anticipation.

A smile with lips pulled towards the ear forewarns of fear or compliance of a fear. In other words, they are accepting a problem.

A frown is indicative of an upset or sadness. It occurs involuntarily because when someone is sad or angry, or upset, the eyebrows will usually be drawn down, causing the mouth to frown. Another such involuntary facial expression involving the mouth is the dropped jaw. When shocked, or surprised, the jaw muscles automatically relax, causing the mouth to open wide.

One of the strongest signs of anger is the narrowed lips, where the red becomes much less visible. Just try to do it when you're not angry— you'll end up looking like Curious George.

Also, if a smile is not genuine, it will end abruptly, as if it didn't know when to stop naturally. It didn't. And a smile should come naturally. Studies have proven that even children who have been blind since birth smile when they are happy.

The Smile on the Mask

"One may smile, and smile, and be a villain," Shakespeare said in *Hamlet*.

We all do it at some time or another. We smile, even when we don't want to, for a smile is not only a sign of humor or pleasure but also of an apology, and, at times, defense. How often do you smile at a boss you do not like, a friend that is giving you a hard time, or a spouse who is driving you up a wall? You bump into someone in the hallway and smile as restitution. But are you really sorry or just trying to make a tense situation more comfortable? Sometimes we use it as armor against an attack.

These smiles have no real significance, except that they are masking what we really mean. Dr. Ewan Grant of Birmingham University coined this as the "oblong smile." He attributes it to the smile we use to be polite. The lips are drawn back from both upper and lower teeth, forming an oblong shape. He adds that this is, "the smile or grimace when one is pretending to enjoy a joke or off-the-cuff remark. Or when a girl gets too much attention from a drunk, or is being chased around the office by the boss."

In *Prison Etiquette,* written by Dr. B. Phillips, he notes that new prisoners are taught to "dogface," to purposely learn to wear an expression that is emotionless. Who does this better than Bond, James Bond? Sean Connery, in my opinion, played the quintessential James Bond in the 007 movies. He rarely reacted, even when someone shot him. What about when a half-naked Miss Pussy Willow handed him a drink, and he didn't blink. (Well, maybe he blinked once.) Nevertheless, Connery mastered the part of a man who remained completely calm, cool, and bloody well emotionless.

But remember, no matter how talented an actor you may be, consistently covering up our inner feelings is difficult at best and virtually impossible at least. Perhaps the face won't give you away, but some part of the body will. A tense situation can cause a person to perspire. Fear can make your hands shake or your legs tremble. Beware of masks and how often a person uses them to make their life easier, as opposed to facing the truth and taking it for what it is worth.

QUIT FROWNING

Frowning is not only unattractive but as most of us know, it can cause wrinkles. But what you probably didn't know is these same scowls can cause headaches. Also, contrary to popular belief, we frown more when we are concentrating than we do when we are angry or upset. So, next time you are focusing, instead of turning your smile upside down, try lifting your eyebrows. The lines on your forehead will be vertical instead of horizontal, thereby eliminating both wrinkles and headaches.

Chins Up

Where did that expression come from? Well, when a person is depressed, sad, confused, or feeling defensive, they tuck their chin in. (Yes, like a chicken—but then you said that, I didn't.) The expression refers to lifting the chin up to normal, not above. If you do, you will give the appearance that you don't have a clue what the other person is talking about. Give it a shot. Next time someone is talking to you, furrow your brows and lift your chin. All of a sudden, they'll start to explain what they just said. Either that or they'll repeat it.

If a person strokes their chin, you can bet you've peaked their interest. Every old western movie features a minor character, usually the doctor, standing around stroking his chin and saying things like, "I don't know if he'll make it or not, Marshall." The "well, let me consider it" gesture may be trite, but true.

BODY BASICS

As Sigmund Freud said, "He who has eyes to see and ears to hear may convince himself that no mortal can keep a secret. If his lips are silent, he chatters with his fingertips. Betrayal oozes out of him at every pore."

Five minutes is all it takes us to size up the average Joe (unless of course he's on television, and then it takes at least five weeks, and why I will never know). Big, small, short, tall, fat, thin, worth talking to, or worth blowing off since a conversation with a total stranger rarely moves beyond small talk, we depend on body language to form our first impression. Unfortunately, it's often our last impression.

Although mastering eye contact, facial expression, and head movements may be vital during this process, they do have certain limitations. The gestures we make often give meaning to the other aspects of non-verbal communication, often where the language ripens and matures to produce much more fruit.

There are certain universal gestures: shaking the fist in anger; clapping as a sign of appreciation; raising one's hand to gain attention; yawning when bored, or patting someone on the back when they've done a good job. Otherwise, the subtleties have such a wide degree of variations in individual movements that it would be virtually impossible to pinpoint them all. And, understand them all. Each carries with it a definite message. But, as they say, the movement is the message—the blueprint of the underlying state of mind of the person at the time. They will be particularly stronger, in most cases, if the feelings are negative—if they are angry, upset, and nervous. It is essential that you recognize this immediately and avoid a potentially emotional disaster. Not that you should be negative, but you must be particularly aware of gestures that set off alarms.

Gerard Nierenberg suggested that gestures are used in expressing openness, defensiveness, readiness, reassurance, frustration, confidence, nervousness, acceptance, expectancy, and lying, just to name a few. They are so predominant in the relationship between our body and mind that we use them even when no one is looking. For example, speaking on the telephone or into a tape recorder.

Words may be the primary persuader in any given situation, but the role of your gestures should never be underestimated. Even when you try not to use them, they may give you away. A stoned faced, poker-playing position, expressing zero emotion, complete with stoic expression and blank eyes, will tell you that the person has something to hide.

Any and every part of the body can be used to make a gesture, and all of them impart some form of communicative value. Even if they are not serious, they reveal something. A man who puffs his chest out with pride will probably look ridiculous, but if he's serious, what does that tell you about him? Another half-serious gesture is sucking the stomach in when in the presence of an attractive woman. Who would not notice this type of movement? Still, if he's serious, take note. The body bellows out a crucial message. Listen carefully.

A Head Above

If you draw back from the face a bit, what you get is a head. Of the game. If you believe the head is moving about randomly, especially if two people are talking, not so. Each nod, shake, pivot, and bounce exposes a naked emotion. For instance, if a man jerked his head back when you spoke, odds are he heard something he didn't like. (Unless of course you slapped him, which would not be displaying the most exemplary behavior.) Obviously, the message offended him in one manner or another. Retract what you said, or at the very least rephrase it.

Thrusting the head forward customarily precedes a challenge of some sort, especially if the thruster feels threatened by the thrustee.

Holding the head high and at an angle indicates superiority. (This does not mean that they are, just that they think they are.) This can also be an expression of aggressiveness, particularly if accompanied by a curled lip or blushing complexion.

A lowered head signifies submissiveness. Japanese women hold their head in this position in front of men, most notably the ones they marry, which probably explains why it can also be a sign of sadness and depression, especially if their voice slows considerably as if they'd eaten a spoonful of peanut butter, or if their posture is slouched.

If a person tilts their head to one side when listening to a speaker, they are genuinely interested in the subject matter. Charles Darwin did numerous studies on animals and men and determined that both would tilt their head slightly when they heard something that pleased them. Dogs do it almost as much as humans (that means my Rosie does). While comprehending a canine presents some difficulties, watch how their ears perk up and they instinctively lean their heads to the side when trying to understand you.

People will nod much more when they are listening, as it unconsciously lets the other person know we are interested and encourages them to open up on the subject to a further degree. Studies have shown that when a listener refuses to nod at all, the speaker can dry up completely, often unable to explain why. On the other hand, continually nodding in an affirmative manner can, and will, drive someone nuts. Being too agreeable is disagreeable. If you are listening to someone and they pause and you want them to continue, you should nod. Just don't nod off.

Bowing the head is a sign of respect, but if the person keeps their head down, perhaps they are looking for hell somewhere down there, as they probably think they are in it. Look for other signs, but basically these people feel dejected.

A person who scratches their head could be puzzled and confused. Or they could have dandruff.

Tossing the head back denotes disdain (although women use this affectation more than men, as a way of attracting attention).

If someone is rocking the head from side to side, they are probably vacillating between two points of view. Like, no kidding right? Worth paying attention to, however.

You'll notice that when people speak, they rarely hold their heads in one position for longer than a sentence. In fact, most of us use head movements as speech markers. Sweeping the head to one side and using blatant chin thrusts places emphasis on a subject or certain words. People habitually lower their head at the end of a statement and raise it at the end of a question. And if a person winks, which is generally considered an eye movement, the head will almost always tilt to the side when doing so, making it a head movement as well. (Unless the wink is on the sly, and then the head will not move at all.) The head is even used to indicate where someone should look. If a person plans to continue speaking but wants a short pause, they will not move their head.

While seated, people will often prop their head in their hands. If the chin is being held by the thumb and first two fingers, this is a good sign of interest. However, if the chin is resting in the palm of the hand, it is more likely a sign of boredom.

The next time you're watching television, turn off the sound and get a head's up on the real conversation. It's amazing what you'll notice. Talking heads.

Shrugging it Off

The supporting actor of our head movements is the shrug. The shrug wants to be the star; however, it can't seem to divest itself of self-doubt. The message is almost always, "I don't know," or "I don't want to know," or "What can I do about it anyway?" So be its fate.

Although it may not seem possible, a single shoulder shrug is worse. The message it portrays even bleaker. The neon signal they are sending is to leave them alone. "Don't touch me," they lament, somewhat bourgeoisie about the whole thing. "Go away." And you should at that point. No purpose will be served by sticking around.

When the chip off the old block won't fall off, some of us have a tendency to shrug it away. It is an unconscious attempt to appear indifferent toward the malady—because we aren't.

In addition, there are those who raise their shoulders above the crowd by keeping them there. They are trying to adopt a position of approachability. "I am not going to harm you in any way," the shoulders say. "So come closer and let me carry the world around for you for awhile." Still, second billing.

Armed with Information

If a person crosses their arms in front of them, it's safe to conclude that they are closing themselves off. One of the ways in which they accomplish this is by making their bodies physically smaller. When you are wrapped around yourself, you literally take up less space, thereby becoming less noticeable, less obtrusive. This is usually because the person perceives themselves as inadequate. They can be quite nervous and tense. If they are holding their body tightly, they are literally trying to get a grip. Someone who closes themselves off like this will not be open to new ideas or information. A good salesperson will not even suggest an offer when their client is in this rather stubborn stance. They continue in a less aggressive manner until the person's arms drop to their side and they appear relaxed.

If they keep their arms uncrossed but their hands folded in front of them, then they haven't decided whether to open up yet or not.

Arms out with elbows bent, and hands placed on the hips or waist, is an extremely confident pose. Definitely an affectation ascertained by an independent person who does not mess around. Also a mannerism used to prevent people from entering into a group or excluding them from one. By taking up more room, and swinging their body away from the person they wish would leave, they literally elbow them out of the picture.

Hands to the chest imply a need for endorsement of the words spoken. They speak "from the heart," more or less.

Holding the arms behind the back is the most open position a person can assume. You can rest assured that they are probably not trying to hide anything and that they are reasonably calm and relaxed. When a soldier is ordered to be "at ease," they relax and hold their hands behind their backs. Politicians and royalty prefer this posture, as they reflect a degree of approachability and honesty. They may be surrounded by bodyguards at the time, yet they wish to convey the idea that they have nothing to fear. Except maybe fear itself.

If this position is assumed with a more erect posture and the chin thrust forward, it's generally a sign of command. Notably so amongst military men. Think of Mussolini and you have the picture. Japanese executives often assume this pose when addressing a group of employees. "I am in control," is what they communicate, and in no uncertain terms.

But if someone places their arms behind their back while clenching their wrist, then they are literally trying to get a hold of themselves. This maneuver lends them a hand while regrouping. Young ingénues routinely assume this position. They get that shy look on their face by dropping their eyes and putting their hands behind their back, swaying the body from side to side gleefully. (If particularly adept at this pseudo-sexy role, a good pout adds to the vulnerability of the moment.) Why? Ah, try it and you'll see. This coquettish gesture causes the breasts to protrude and appear larger.

(Unless of course you are a man, and then it will only succeed in making you look gay.)

Give Yourself a Hand

Hands down, the winner of the most honest, open position is when the hand is offered with the palm up, fingers outstretched. Why? It's a vulnerable gesture, thereby allowing the recipient a veritable (or more likely virtual) guarantee that the person can be sensitive to someone else's needs. On the other hand, if someone shows you the back of theirs, it means they want to take control and are not open to argument.

The second best position is hands flat on the table, especially when closing a deal. (Other good indications that go hand in hand here, are putting down a pen or pencil, pushing the papers away, or shutting a folder or briefcase.)

I worked with a man who constantly played with his wedding band. Needless to say, he filed for a divorce within weeks, finally removing it all together. Then he lost it. What does that tell you? If a person plays with their wedding ring, especially if they keep sliding it up and down their finger, or removing it and replacing it, subconsciously, or consciously, they have marital issues that they should explore. Otherwise, fiddling with rings, and moving the hands restlessly, indicates nervousness and/or embarrassment.

Hiding your hands, such as placing them under the table or in your pockets, substantiates a hidden agenda. You are definitely holding something back.

If a man's hands cling to something (i.e., the arms of a chair), he may be literally trying to get a grip. If you are speaking while he does this, chances are he doesn't like what he's hearing.

Forming a fist with the hands is generally a sign of anger, especially if the fist is being shaken in your face. Beware, for even if they are conversing calmly, they are upset, angry, or plain just don't like you. If the thumb is hidden within that fist, then they feel threatened as well. This is also a sign of stubbornness, and you will have a hard time convincing them of just about anything. Charles Darwin noted in his book, *Expression of Emotion in Man and Animal*, that the clenched fist signified anger but also determination. He also went on to add that a man gesturing with his fist will also force his opponent to clench his fist in retaliation. This, Darwin noted, will naturally result in a heated argument or other display of hostility.

The palm to the back of the neck verifies a pain in one. This is not just defensive but a beaten, defensive position. Next time you attend a sporting event, watch the coach on the team that is losing. You may often see him slumping slightly with one hand behind his neck. If they miss a play, an athlete will often assume this position immediately after removing his helmet.

But now if both hands are behind the head, it is a definite sign of superiority, in which the other person adopts an apathetic approach to you or what you are saying. Basically, they are suggesting that they are too important to deign to listen to you, but you should listen to them. Your feelings are incidental.

Cut someone off in traffic and watch what they do. A few may give you the finger, with the exception of New York, where everyone will. Those that don't will invariably stick their finger under their collar instead. Anger makes our blood pressure rise and consequently our body temperature along with it. Hot under the collar is not just a quaint expression.

Excessive touching of the face, especially around the mouth, speaks of dishonesty about the subject matter. This stems back to our childhood. Children unconsciously cover their mouths after they've told a lie. Many of us carry this habit into adulthood by trying to "cover-up" what was said.

Steepling our fingers together like a church makes a person appear more intelligent. The trouble is when you go to great lengths to appear intelligent and in control, you often come off as arrogant and impudent. The higher the steeple on the face, the more superior the person may feel. For instance, fingers can be steepled in the lap (more a sign of pensive contemplation), to a steeple under the chin (superiority in their knowledge), to steepling that touches the forehead (they find that they are far above this conversation, or you).

Pointing a finger can mean "you," or it could be signaling a direction. Either way it's rude. Listen to your mother. Don't point.

Almost everyone knows that a finger to the lips means, "be quiet," so we'll shut up about it.

Drumming your fingers, or twiddling your thumbs, can only mean one thing: borrrrrrring. Sure signs of insecurity are fidgeting and touching your hair excessively. And biting your nails, or picking at your cuticles, are dead giveaways for someone who is nervous and stressed out.

Talking with your hands is natural. Getting carried away is not. (You know, the type that knocks the glass over at the dinner table.) In this case, big, wide movements are distracting and frustrating, not to mention messy. If you're not sure if you have a tendency to do this, then watch yourself in a mirror next time you talk on the telephone. Chances are you use many of the same hand movements. So, if you see yourself picking at your cuticles with your teeth, you may do this in person without realizing it.

Touching an object proclaims possession. Take a look at a picture of a man standing beside his new boat, home, car, wife, you name it. Invariably, he will be touching his new prized possession, because how else would he announce to the world that it belongs to him? If somebody walks into your home, or your office, and picks up an object and begins examining it, or fondling it, take it back. They are saying that this could belong to them. Either that or they are just nosy busybodies. Do not allow this. Whatever they are touching belongs to you and you belong to you.

If a man hitches his pants up, he has just made a decision of some sort. Isn't this generally the case when you see a man doing this?

Clattering change in the pocket is shaking up a preoccupation with money. It's a sign that no matter how much they have, it isn't enough. I read somewhere that the famed movie mogul, Louis B. Mayer, had a habit of jingling his coins in his hand, especially when making a deal with a large amount of money at stake. Beggars are aware of the importance of the sound that money makes. They jingle the jars as much as possible while holding them out towards you. Hmmm . . . could there be a connection?

Handshakes
<u>Handshakes</u>

Handshakes originated from the need to show fellow citizens that they weren't carrying a weapon. The gesture began as both hands in the air (as in put your hands up, which is where that originated). Later, this evolved into one hand in the air with the other placed on the chest. "See, no knife up my sleeve." Obviously, there's no need for such extremities anymore, and the handshake matured into a sign of respect, with the palms interlocking to imply openness and touching to declare oneness.

Handshakes should be firm, not bone crushing, and, optimally, your hand should be dry and warm. Being offered a limp, damp hand is not an auspicious beginning. This is known as the dead fish handshake and leads people to believe you are pretty much drowning. Also, if your palms are perspiring, they may be right. If your hands are damp or cold, try running hot or cold water on your wrists just before the meeting. The wrists are more sensitive and control the temperature in your body.

Do not claw or paw your way into a handshake. This denotes that there is no heart in your hand and is most often associated with people who are greedy and trying to grab what they can from you.

The political candidate's handshake is equally as inappropriate, even for political candidates, if you ask me. However they seem to continuously get away with it, despite being advised that this is a greeting reserved for very close friends. The candidate's handshake: grasping a hand with their right hand and cupping it with their left (or touching the person's forearm or upper arm can be substituted). With a stranger, the gesture comes off as if they are trying too hard by falsely ingratiating themselves. Hah!

A weak handshake usually denotes a weak character. If someone grabs the tip of your fingers, or his or her hand goes limp in yours, then the person could possibly be having a hard time connecting with you—or doesn't want to connect with you. Whether they are aware of it or not, they feel uncomfortable and ill at ease.

Men are often not sure how to shake a woman's hand. As is the rule, the handshake should remain firm, yet comfortable. In other words, if he shakes her hand too hard, he's likely to be domineering and aggressive, whereas if his handshake is weak he may lack strength of character. So, appearing gentlemanly, with a soft touch, can be self-defeating, not to mention insulting.

A friendly, confident handshake is taut, not tight. It comes at you straight, not from above coming down or below coming up. Straight.

A KISS IS NOT JUST A KISS!

The handshake is not the most common manner of greeting. Actually, the kiss endears more cultures and societies. Mexicans kiss once on the cheek. Egyptians kiss three times, one on each cheek, then back to the first. Italians kiss four times, two smooches on each cheek. In Polynesia, men and women will lean forward and rub noses gently, as do Eskimos. And, despite what one might think, the French don't pucker up with a total stranger; they traditionally prefer a light embrace, followed by a hug on either side of the chest. Some of this may be imprecise but is not without general validity.

<u>Legs and Feet</u>

Ah, feet. As in life, if you keep them planted firmly on the ground, you can't go wrong. If they are together and facing you directly, so much the better. You can be sure the person is not only forthright, but also well-balanced.

Feet jiggling, or tapping, is as annoying as drumming your fingers. Not only does this convey boredom but it also gives the impression that you just can't wait to run out of there.

On your toes? This is a "sprint" position. Someone is looking for a way out, fast. If seated, the person often adapts this same strategy by positioning their feet under their chair.

Wrapping one foot around the leg is generally a telltale sign that the person is nervous, and uncomfortably so. That or they have to go to the bathroom. It doesn't matter what else they are doing or saying, deep down inside you can bet they are a basket case.

Locking ankles is another sure sign that the person may be holding back, either emotionally or intellectually, by not supplying all of the information you need. This gesture also signifies stress. Next time you're on an airplane, take a look around. During takeoffs and landings, passengers are more apt to cross their ankles.

If a man sits with his legs apart, he will most likely be confident and secure. For women, it's not usually recommended, but if she sits with her knees touching and legs together, feet pointed toward the person with whom she is conversing, she will appear extremely self-assured. Now if he assumes the same position, but his feet are pointing away, he may want to get the heck out of there in a hurry. (Check to see if his body is pointed toward the door. If so, he'd rather leave than listen.)

Want to tell if a man is from Europe or not? During World War II more American intelligence officers were captured because they failed to cross their legs like a European. What am I talking about? European men cross one leg over the other. A vast majority of American men find this "effeminate" and will cross the leg horizontally with the ankle resting on the opposite knee. It's a dead giveaway. (So is the fact that American men have a tendency to hold their forks in their right hand. An error the Armed Force's later rectified.)

Someone who sits with one leg under the other is usually pretty free-spirited. They don't much care what people think of them, especially you, which is why you will often see children sitting in this manner.

Legs stretched out in front of you imply dominance. I once made the mistake of sitting in this manner at a Siddah Yoga lesson. I was strongly reprimanded by the Master for putting my feet out in front of me and pointing them directly at the teacher. I was sitting on the floor, so I thought it was okay. I was asked to leave.

If a person's foot is constantly resting on the heel, guess what? They could well be one.

MESSAGES IN MOTION

No longer is posturing relegated to the ranks of models prancing around with books on their heads. So important has the role of body language become to our personality and character that it is one of the first things a psychiatrist will look at. Signs of depression are most evident in the way a person stands and moves. Often, they will have shrinking body movements, as if hiding themselves, and they will frequently jerk when they move. Their shoulders slump and they have a look of resignation about them. If a person looks like they are carrying the weight of the world on their shoulders, they usually are. Their shoulders become rounded, and they lean into their chest. Remember, when you repress one area, you repress others as well. These patients are often diagnosed with heart trouble or lung problems.

Oddly enough, people who have gone through long periods of depression and recovered fully will still assume the same position they held when they were ill. They will often slouch and sag, years later. Doctors found that working with patients to improve their posture, and change their old habits regarding it, also improved their attitudes and relationships.

We each have our own unique repertoire of postures that we use on a daily basis. In fact, a friend can pick you out in a crowd simply by the way you are standing. Posture plays such an important role in communicating emotions or attitudes, not only about ourselves but also how we feel about other people. Research has recently shown that people often adopt a different posture when they are speaking with their mother than they do when speaking with their father. So much so, that even if you cannot see which parent they may be conversing with, you'd be able to distinguish between the two.

People in a group will stand differently if they are accepted than if not. Outsiders will stand with the weight on one foot, while insiders will lean into the center.

Snapping the head forward is a forceful motion. If they lunge when they walk as well, they are usually angry and hostile. Check to see if their fists are clenched.

If being forced to listen, or if a person is disinterested in the subject matter, they will lean back and turn their head away from the speaker.

If someone doesn't like you, he or she may do a number of things. But, consistently, one mannerism manifests more than any other. They will stand straighter. That's because standing too straight, in a rigid manner, makes them appear inflexible in their decisions. Much like an exclamation point. They see things one way and one way only and will not tolerate it if you disagree. Maintaining this position consistently over a period of time constitutes an authoritative and snobbish person. They like things orderly and neat and have a difficult time functioning outside of their own familiar parameters. This type of stick in the mud can be a real pain in the butt.

Standing with the hands on the hips is a sign of wanting to participate. Next time you're watching a sporting event, notice the athletes standing in the sidelines. They often adopt this posture, with their hands on their hips, legs slightly apart (it's hard to stand with your hands on your hips without spreading the legs a bit), anxiously waiting to be called into action. Men will take this position when they want to let someone know they are interested, that they are ready to come over and get to know you. In this case, the thumbs will usually be hitched into the pants waist or pockets. At a business meeting, someone taking this stance is asking that you follow in their footsteps. They believe in what they are saying and are genuinely enthusiastic. My daughter takes this position when I ask her to clean her room, or clean anything for that matter. In defiance, we often want to stand our ground, and our hands to our hips position us more securely.

People who put their feet up on their desk, or on the bottom drawer, or any other piece of furniture, are literally trying to get a leg up. They are confident and extremely ambitious. In a story in the March 2004 issue of *Elle Magazine,* the writer observes, "…stare curiously, as do I, at a very sleepy Paris Hilton, the 23-year-old heiress to a share of the estimated $300 million hotel family fortune who has kicked off her lavender suede Steve Madden ankle boots and propped up her white-sweat-socked size 11 feet on a rococo vanity." That about says it all.

If someone poses for you, or you feel they are, leave. They are insecure and disingenuous, not to mention self-centered. Apparently, they think the world revolves around them, and that would include you.

A confident posture hits you straight on. (The back is straight, the head straight). They will distribute their weight evenly on both feet and have a generally open stance. The same goes if they are seated. The back will be straight, the head erect, and the weight will be on both feet pointed directly in front of them or at the person to whom they are speaking. This lends them a sense of security. What could possibly make a person more approachable?

Walking Away

Walking happens to be one of the few forms of body language that changes most dramatically with our moods. Even children move more quickly and are "light on their feet," when they are happy. When upset, they walk as if someone put lead in their shoes. Even as we grow older, if we feel dejected, we scuffle along and don't look up.

You'll notice that when people walk with their heads raised high and their arms swinging, chests protruding and legs rigid, they think they are better than anyone else. The worst job I ever had was at a law firm, where my boss, who was one of the attorneys with his name on the door, walked like this. This was typically how Benito Mussolini strutted his stuff. He raised his chin, swung his arms in an exaggerated motion, and his pace calculated to impress. His followers did just that. They followed. As a sign of respect and loyalty, those in charge guide the rest. The FBI did hundreds of studies on this very fact because this class structuring actually helped them to determine who was "boss" during Mafia meetings. The top man always walked slightly in front of his subordinates.

People who walk rapidly with their hands on their hips are trying to get somewhere quickly—mostly in their minds, even though their feet take the brunt of the beating. Their short burst of energy is followed by a pensive pose that's almost sluggish. Sir Winston Churchill walked in this manner. He frequently walked with his head down and his hands behind him. Anyone that adopts this slow and deliberate pace is deep in thought and usually contemplating a problem.

People who are timid and weak have a tendency to slouch. They want to appear noninvasive, and they will often walk so softly you might think they were walking on eggshells. That's because they are.

Okay, ladies, if you want to walk away from a man in style, here's how you do it: Confident people have an even pace, with a slight bounce to their walk. They look at other people and smile. Their posture is straight, with their head up and arms swinging at their sides in an easy and relaxed manner. Now walk on by.

ENTERING THE ZONE

Just like animals, humans have territories, boundaries around their own personal space. Worse, they carry it around with them everywhere they go.

Different cultures have different parameters for their perimeters. (When traveling, it's always best to learn the local customs regarding space, handshakes, and etiquette.) The Japanese, Latinos, and Middle Easterners all stand closer (roughly ten inches apart), than most Westerners. As a rule, most Americans prefer eighteen inches around them during a one-on-one confrontation with a stranger. In a crowd, Americans are even less tolerant, where studies indicate they prefer six to eight square inches per person, and if space permits, a good ten feet in all directions.

Standing too close to a person can cause physical changes in their body. Their blood pressure rises and their heart pumps quicker, sending a burst of adrenaline rushing through the body. They react much the way they would to anyone else intruding upon their space, including a burglar. If you don't retreat, you leave them with a negative impression, and they are less likely to want to be up close and personal with you again.

Establishing boundaries is common even when seated. At their desk, a worker will frequently stretch papers to the edges to keep their workspace private.

Police interrogators are well aware of the personal space invasion technique. A textbook on criminal interrogation trains officers to sit close to their suspect, preferably eliminating any obstacles between them, such as a table or another chair, which could potentially provide a degree of relief. They suggest the officer begin with their chair two to three feet away, inching it closer and closer as the interview intensifies, until they are literally in the suspect's face. By then his confidence and self-assurance should be nonexistent.

People who continually approach from the side are usually not to be trusted. They are literally sidling up beside you in a conspiratorial manner. I am not kidding when I write this (observe for yourself) that politicians do this more often than anyone else.

Freud clearly understood the need for personal space by having his patients lie on a couch while he sat in a chair placed out of their sight, thereby being the least intrusive. (He also noted that as a rule people reflect better while in a prone position and create better when in a vertical one.)

Not surprisingly, powerful people take up more space. Status seekers employ this device on purpose. Whether by the accouterments they wear or carry with them, or the entourage surrounding them, or by simply extending their arms often, they have mastered the art of bigger is better in any and all areas, including the one they occupy at the moment.

You'll notice this when someone guards his or her territory. Bodyguards and bouncers are notorious for assuming this pose—shoulders pulled back, legs apart, feet firmly planted, hands on hips and arms folded in front of them. It makes them appear bigger and stronger.

Even lovers, who are obviously the most tolerant as far as proximity goes (one would hope), have limits to their territorial orientation. Don't most people close their eyes when they kiss? We spend so much time getting close, and then when we are, we shut our eyes. Perhaps it is because even when we are intimate, we must maintain our own illusion of separateness.

The sexual link allows for another exception to the rule. If a woman moves into a man's territory, she will encounter less resistance than a man moving into a woman's territory. A man will be less likely to resent the intrusion as a means for a possible sexual encounter, while a woman is simply put on her guard. Another interesting observation is that women talking to other women will stand closer than men talking to other men.

What is the height of a man's tolerance level, an important issue even if you aren't one? Among wolves, the pack leader asserts his dominance by wrestling another wolf to the ground and then standing over it. The "loser" will then roll onto his back in defeat, and then crawl away in subservience. A tall person, aware of this intimidation, will sit down during business meetings to equal his stature with his colleagues. Conversely, a boss will enter his employee's office without knocking, come in half way, and remain standing. Or the boss that crowds up on the side of his employee will catch his employee off guard and make him feel insecure.

Where a person chooses to place himself within the confines of a limited territory can be quite revealing. For instance, if someone wishes to remain obscure, they gravitate toward one of the corners of the room, usually the one farthest from the door. At a table, they will do the same, picking the seat in a corner as far from the door as possible. Studies have proven that a jurist who chooses the head of the table will almost always be chosen as the foreman. A truly aggressive person will pick the center of things to claim as his own. The table, the room, it doesn't matter; he'll be right in the thick of things. These people will face the door, challenging those that enter.

How can you tell if you have inadvertently crossed a person's line? Well, assuming they don't leave, they may lean back or fold their arms in front of them. Tucking their chin into their chest is also an indication that they are trying to "protect" themselves. When placed in a situation where the person cannot turn away, such as a crowded elevator, bus or train, they will invariably turn their head in the least offensive direction, thereby avoiding eye contact. They will remain rigid and make as few movements as possible. Back off!

EXCEPTIONS TO THE RULE

Culture plays such a strong role in body language that it definitely needs to be addressed. No matter where you live, or where you are from, you must be sensitive to another person's background. If you are not open to learning about another culture, then any language will ultimately elude you.

Being aware of territorial differences is essential, as mentioned above. Certain universal gestures can be distinguished accurately across the world. People smile when they are happy and scowl when they are mad. At the same time, there are hundreds of gestures unique to certain countries. For a Japanese man to lick a forefinger and stoke an eyebrow would be one way for him to indicate that the person he is conversing with is a liar. In India, it is quite common for people to nod their head up and down when they mean no and from side to side when they mean yes. A thumbs-up in Italy means number one, but in Greece, it can be very rude indeed.

Whether you see it this way or not, eye contact is also an ethnic trait. Greeks, for instance, look at people more often and more intently than any other culture. Swedish people are more reserved and have been found to look at strangers or mild acquaintances less often. Arabs like to look people directly in the eye when conversing, where the Japanese have a tendency to focus on a person's neck or shoulders.

Not surprisingly, Americans and the Brits have fewer and less expressive facial movement. (And who would have guessed that Italians are the most expressive when conversing?) Also, as you'd anticipate by now, the Japanese use few facial expressions in public. They are more generous with smiles, however, especially when greeting people.

As for touching people, Latinos take the prize. They touch more than any other race, except for perhaps Arabs. It is not unusual to see Arab men holding hands in public as a sign of friendship. Arab women, however, are not touched at all in public. Period.

There may be geographical reasons why a person speaks the way they do. New Yorkers will speak much faster than the locals in Hawaii. Or, their voice may have a nasal twang to it if they live in the South. Accent the area before drawing conclusions.

Medical conditions should also be taken into consideration. Listen to Muhammad Ali or Michael J. Fox and the difference in their speech patterns due to Parkinson's disease. A jaw abnormality may cause stuttering, even lisping. If someone has a hearing problem they often talk too loudly, making him or her appear rude, even obnoxious. They may also have a difficult time pronouncing the *r* or *s* sound. How many people do you know that are self-conscious of their teeth? I know a few who won't open their mouths fully when they speak. They virtually never smile and when they do, it's more of a Cheshire cat kind of smile that makes it appear to be contrived and phony.

Clothing, makeup, accessories, hygiene, all of these aspects of a person's personality are important and, for the most part, pretty obvious, but there are too many variables to jump to conclusions. If, however, a man wears a baseball hat night and day because he's balding, he has issues. A woman who wears her hair down to her waist isn't unusual, but if she's over fifty and completely gray, she's making a statement. They both have a fear of aging. Sometimes, they don't even know they have this fear. Some people get caught in a time warp and still think of themselves at a certain age for the rest of their lives. They can be forty and continue dressing the way they did in high school. It takes a big wake up call for them to see who and what they've really become.

I have met men with loud voices who are extremely gentle and men with nervous twitches who were extremely secure. If you want to read people accurately, you must gather enough information. Be aware of everything— the surrounding, the circumstances, the person's socioeconomic background and emotional maturity. And don't be fooled. If a person changes their behavior abruptly, check to see if they are under stress or if they haven't been feeling well. There's a big difference between having a bad attitude and having a bad hair day.

Talk about confusing. The point is it would be impossible to learn, or even understand, every nuance in every nation. The trick is to follow up with additional evidence. Consider each of a person's characteristics in light of the circumstances. Are these characteristics controllable or a permanent quality? Look for extremes in behavior. Once you've gathered enough data, then and only then should you determine the meaning of the mannerisms.

CLUSTERS OF CLUSTERS

There's an old Cantonese proverb that goes something like, "Beware of the man whose stomach doesn't move when he laughs."

When trying to understand what someone is saying without saying it, keep that proverb in mind. Certain movements just go together. When we're communicating, we usually use several different methods to get the point across. One shift in body weight is not a sign of anything. Nor is one twitch of an eye, one wave of a hand in the air, or one deep gulp of a swallow. If someone is not interested in what you have to say, they will not just glance away. They will glance away and then fold their arms in front of them. If that doesn't work, they will move their body at an angle away from you, usually pointing towards the door.

Ditto if they like you. You may see a man return your gaze, then narrow his eyes. Do you have his attention, or does he have vision problems? Wait and see if he responds with more clusters. If he turns towards you, lowers his arms, stands straight and smiles, well, then he's definitely showing signs of interest.

To say simply that a single body position holds significance would be naïve, and justified spuriously. Rubbing the nose with one finger doesn't necessarily mean that the person is rejecting what you said, or that patting is a sure sign or approval, or steepling the fingers is a sign of superiority. Do not take one movement out of context, and remember to rely upon the overall picture.

A man who keeps his arms crossed while you are speaking to him is clearly saying, "I am not willing to open my mind up to what you are saying. I am not willing to go along with you." And he's pretty adamant about it, too. Rather than go on speaking, which by the way will do you absolutely no good, you should look for other ways in which he is communicating. If his face is closed as well, usually by drawing his eyebrows together and narrowing his eyes, it could well be that what he means to communicate is, "I don't mind you coming over and talking to me, I want to talk back, but I feel trapped, and I can't get out of this closed up position I am in." Two completely different stories. Exhaust all methods for drawing your conclusion before doing so.

Gesture-clusters indicate, from movement to movement, an overall response. In each moment, you can then learn how the information you are trying to put across is being received. Speakers often use this technique to see how well the audience is relating. Are they open or defensive? Bored and wishing they could leave? They taper their speech accordingly. They will change the pace, withdraw, or change their approach to get the audience back. Being aware of clusters is being aware of feedback.

Usually one gesture will trigger another, and with a combination of two or more, you can safely evaluate the situation. Otherwise, all you may have is the wallflower that accidentally got drunk at the punch bowl.

CHAPTER SEVEN

POINTS, PLANES, AND PRESENTATION

In any given situation in your life, you are doing one of two things: you are either participating or you are observing. Observing can teach you a lot about a person as we've been talking about; however, it's not the most advantageous position to put yourself in. Participating, especially in a conversation, gets you more involved. And in this case, involvement is power. How? You can take control of a conversation by grabbing the reins and steering it in the right direction. If something doesn't sound right, delve a bit deeper until you differentiate between fact and what could well be fiction. If a man skips around a topic, you can revisit it later. Verbal voodoo will no longer have you under its spell. Simply by understanding the right questions to ask, and the right delivery, you have mastered the art of involvement.

What if they won't allow you to drive? Consider the passenger. There's a definite reason people volunteer certain information, while simultaneously avoiding other subjects. What does the person attempt to accomplish by not responding? Is he trying to extract facts from you, or is he hiding something he doesn't want you to find out about? Pursue the conversation until you find out.

How exactly do you do this? First, you have to make a man comfortable enough to open up, by...

BUILDING RAPPORT

It doesn't matter how astute you become at posing the proper questions if you can't make a man comfortable enough to respond. No one will confide in someone who readily judges or condemns them. We confide in those who accept us, those with whom we have some kind of commonality, unless they wear a long black robe and sit behind a drawn curtain. Besides our pious fathers or mothers, we must feel equal in order to acknowledge that our souls are as steeped in secrets as Krispy Crèmes are steeped in grease. Once you gain a man's attention, it's up to you to compel them, inferentially, to focus on the donut and not the hole.

If they are standing with their arms folded like an old-fashioned cigar-store Indian, then you deduce that they are not open to anything you have to say. Fold your arms as well. Then be warm and fuzzy by utilizing eye contact and smiling frequently. Give the person your full interest, making it clear that they may take as much of your time as necessary. Slowly, unfold your arms into an open position and see if they follow suit. If so, you have succeeded in peeling away the first layer of lame excuses they could have presented you with at this point in time, such as I have to go because it's more fun to watch the grass grow. You have met upon common ground. Mush! Continue onward.

Rapport means being able to relate to someone on their terms, through your actions, your conversations. You must figure out what makes them tick, and why they think the way they do. In order to do this, you must establish common values and interests. Get them involved in the discussion by motivating them to contribute. Reduce any anxiety and defensiveness by permitting them to set the pace and style of the interaction. Most of us do this naturally when trying to get to know someone new, we just never realized why. The ability to do this consciously and quickly can be more powerful than you ever suspected.

SELF-DISCLOSURE

One of the easiest and most expedient ways in which to put someone at ease is self-disclosure. "Yes, I know how you feel because I have felt that way, too," instantaneously promotes you from the status of enemy to coconspirator. You understand. And, if a man understands that you understand, he tends be more forthright about divulging his inner most secrets. Doesn't matter if it's about bucking broncos or current interest rates, what establishes the candor is a connection. Chemical dialogue between brain transmitters. Questions flare, and, hopefully, answers explode. Again, move cautiously. Moving in fits and starts through the midtown traffic of a man's mind is not only precautionary, but wise. Jumping from general questions to penetrating inquiries about his parents' marriage and how many children he would like to have someday will kill a conversation.

Volunteer information about yourself, but do not get too familiar too fast. Edge into your personal life without revealing too much. Balance is the key to self-disclosure. Attorneys master the art. They debrief potential jurors, not to mention secretly deriding them, using this technique. He talks to the potential juror as if they are sitting in his living room. The attorney has prepared questions to determine his objective. He then lets just enough information slip out, convincing the juror to drop his defenses. Unconsciously, the juror appreciates the fact that the attorney empathizes with him, thereby encouraging openness and honesty.

Not only can you use self-disclosure verbally but non-verbally as well. Increase your gestures and change your body posture often (in a friendly manner, of course). Use mirroring techniques (discussed later), as often as possible. But basically allow him to dominate the content of the conversation, and use disclosure accordingly.

THE RIGHT QUESTIONS FOR THE RIGHT ANSWERS

The single most powerful way to destroy a relationship is to stop communicating. You stop communicating when you stop talking, and you stop talking when you stop asking questions. Asking meaningful questions is what keeps you in touch with someone's mind, and listening to the answers is what keeps you in touch with their heart. You'll never understand anyone until you know how to ask intelligent questions and decipher the answers.

Man-ese can be easily understood, if one doesn't read into the words, only between them.

In the beginning stages of a relationship, it is critical to ask the right questions and interpret the answers effectively and accurately. How else could you determine if you can meet a man's expectations, and more importantly, if they can meet yours? Essentially, you must escort your man in the direction of your main concerns. And, make certain there are no collisions along the way.

One way to accomplish this is to ask about his friends. Who is his best friend, and why? You'll be surprised how many adults hesitate when answering this question or don't have an answer at all. This can be quite telling in and of itself. If appropriate, take a nosedive into his past relationships. Did he drown in the relationship? Who broke up with whom? Is he still clinging to the lifeboat, hoping his ex will fish him out?

No matter how you swim around in the murky waters of a man's mind, basically you're trying to figure out how he handled the whole male/female role. For instance, is he afraid of commitment? Well, if you've discovered that he's in his forties and never been married, never lived with anyone, and his longest relationship lasted a couple of years (and they lived in different cities), you can kind of conclude that this may be the case. Unless you're willing to dedicate a lot of time to figuring out what exactly he's afraid of, you can move on.

Still, regardless of how many questions you ask and how many varied answers you receive, there's really only one that counts. This will probably shock you, as it's not a question to ask of him. It is a question to ask yourself. How does he make *you* feel? It seems obvious, but take a second, and ask yourself what you experience when he is around. Open the doorway to your mind; don't just peek inside. In fact, if you can muster the guts, run inside the room and take a good look around before you make a mad dash back. Happy? Sad? Disgusted? Hateful? Loved? Bored?

The next question? If this person upsets you, for whatever reason, then you have to ask yourself why they are still a part of your life. Insecurity? Fear? Only you can determine if you like that particular personality type and how it affects you emotionally. Only you can determine whether or not that person should remain in your life.

Preparing Questions

At this juncture, the reader is fated to hear a little story. More of an anecdote, really; however, at times fiction precedes fact. It is said that a celebrated French mystic, by the name of Mlle. Le Normand, left such an imprint on history that anymore than a cursory introduction would insult the Europeans, most especially the French. Who does not know of her name? Well, that would be mois. Until recently. I, in my many travels, found an account of her faux famed celebrity, in which reference was made of her unprecedented predictions for the great Napoleon, memorializing his phenomenal rise and sudden fall, before they even occurred.

Apparently, he came to her one night when the moon was as big and brassy as one of his concubines (now that's not true, but it sounded good), and asked her if a great battle would be won. She consulted her cards, and after much deliberation, announced brightly that yes the great battle would be won. She was right, of course, the great battle was won. Unfortunately, it was not won by Napoleon Bonaparte.

Questions can be extremely ambiguous. Before a meeting of any kind, take the time to consider the ideal inquiry. Be precise. Be clear. Be illuminating. If you don't know what you want to know, make it mandatory that you figure it out. If you prepare your questions in advance, you most likely will. By drawing a road map of where you want to go, you can expect to reach your destination. Otherwise, you may well end up in Timbuktu. With somebody else.

Now allow me to be a bit more exact. Humor me. You do not have to pull out index cards one after the other. He does not need to be Jay Leno-ed. You don't even have to write the questions down. Just keep the main points foremost in your mind. Remain clear about what information you wish disclosed. If you're divorced with children, seeking a long-term relationship, then your questions should revolve around his attitude towards children. Asking a man if he likes children is a lot different than asking him if he likes being around children. You want to uncover information. That's what questions are for.

Most people listen with the intent to respond. By being prepared, you can focus on other crucial clues, like body language, voice intonations, etc.

Three things to remember when preparing questions:

1. Make the question specific. Asking if he likes flowers is not as telling as asking what his favorite flower is.
2. Try to avoid using compound questions. Two-parted questions are tricky. Generally speaking, a person will answer one part or the other, not both. And, if they do choose to address both, the answer is diluted with the diversity.
3. Make your questions relevant.

Do not act like a reporter. The best way to avoid sounding as if you are interrogating someone is to mix in a few open-ended questions to keep the chat going. What was it like growing up on a farm? This will help you gain insight into his background without sounding like you are prying. Go with the flow, slowly and tactfully, beginning with the basics. Watch for signs that you may be getting too personal, too quickly. If his eyes start wandering around the room, if he fidgets in his chair, shifts weight, or turns his body away, then regroup and begin again.

What subjects should you center on? Good question. Three areas you should focus on are his background, his satisfaction with life in general, and his long-term goals. For example:

- Where were you born and raised? What planet did you grow up on?
- Did your mom help you with your homework?
- Did you play Little League?
- What did your parents do for a living?
- Were you close to your brothers and sisters? Are you close to them now?
- What did you want to be when you grew up? (We're assuming the guy is grown up now.)
- Do you like your job?

Steer him along until you have explored the subject to your satisfaction. For instance, if he is not doing now what he originally set out to do for a living, find out why. There must be a reason.

Avoid argumentative questions, as they serve no purpose. A person simply gets mad and leaves, or they agree with you. Reluctant admission is pointless. They are telling you what you want to hear to get you to shut up. No politics, no religion on the first date. You're asking for trouble.

When you ask questions, the pitch of your voice will naturally become higher at the end. "Where are you going?" The voice will naturally rise on *ing*. But that's usually not the only thing that will rise. Watch a man's head lift slightly at the end of the question. And if you pay close attention, you will notice that people often raise a hand at the same time. People will rarely stay in the same position when asking questions, because emotions fluctuate with a change in topic. So, having said that, if a person remains motionless, it usually means that they really don't care to answer.

What was the Question Again?

A word about people who answer questions with a question. Don't you hate them? I do. They drive me crazy. Take heed of the motives here. It doesn't always mean they are being evasive, although usually they are. When someone answers in this manner, they are tossing the ball back in your court. They are being non-committal and want your stance on the subject first. Yes-men types do this all the time. They are eager to please, thereby tailoring the answer to fit what you want to hear.

If the question they use to counter yours is completely unrelated, then they are attempting to redirect the conversation. Or being secretive. Try to guide them back on course.

If they are trying to clarify your original question, repeat it back to them. To avoid sounding rude, rephrase the question, or move on and go back to it later.

Is there a long pause between your question and the answer? The sudden narcoleptic pause counts against them. They have difficulty answering, obviously, because they do not want to lie, or divulge the truth. Either sucks. Don't push it. But do revert back to the subject at a later date (before you are married). It's always acceptable to toss a wrench into a person's cognitive machinery. Do not say something like, "I'm sorry, I don't remember if I asked you this, but what was your first job?" Reexamine without reestablishing last contact.

If there's still a long pause, or they stop talking completely, therein lies a potential problem. In addition, if they appear anxious and start acting like wires crossed in their head that would generally be the case. Our voices tend to get knotted up along with our wiring. There's been a momentary glitch in the system. It could be he's surprised, or perhaps offended. Look for signs. If he exhales and turns his head away then he's frustrated. If his jaw clenches, he's mad. Don't try to fill the void. Go back to safe ground. Talk about something he enjoyed discussing earlier then move forward in a different direction.

Listening is more Important than Hearing

Studies show that we speak at a rate of approximately 150 to 160 words per minute but listen at a rate of 650 to 700 words per minute. That's giving us a lot of time to evaluate, reject, contest, or agree with what we hear. This also supplies us with ample time to interrupt. Don't. Verbal hand grenades (yeah, you know . . .), physical molatove cocktails (flipping one hand upward and letting it fall), and emotional bombs (big, wet sigh) can blow a conversation to pieces. Aside from that, it's rude.

So, what do you do if a man is mouthing off? Let 'em. One of the keys to gaining information lies in the ability to allow a torrent of verbiage to spill out verbatim. All types of gems can be found hidden in the outpour. Hopefully, rambling on endlessly is not a habit, as this could present quite a predicament—see how to spot a liar.

Remember that it becomes virtually impossible to listen when you are talking yourself, or talking to yourself. Do not sit there contemplating the many intelligent responses you can come up with to counter his comments. Do not think about what you're going to say or ask next. Do not think about the meaning behind his words. *Oh yes, they are saying that, but this is what I think they really mean.* They'll be plenty of time for that later.

And, please eliminate the "yeah, buts" from the conversation. "Yeah, but," will break anyone's thought process, as you automatically interjected a negative. Whether you realize it or not, and whether the person you're speaking to realizes it or not, *but* is a negative qualifier. It means that you do not agree with the first part of what was said. Replace the word *but* with *and.* "I like that restaurant, and . . . " sounds so much nicer than, "I like that restaurant, but . . . "

Obviously, you don't want to appear obvious. Frequently, when we try to listen too carefully, we make people uncomfortable. One of the most common reactions is to stare into the other person's eyes and not let them go. And that is death to the questioner. The other person will clam up.

When and Where to Ask

Have you ever noticed how newlyweds argue a lot? Nine times out of ten, it's because they don't know when to pick their fights. They start demanding answers to questions at the end of the day, when they are both tired and stressed out, or in the morning when they are both tired and stressed out.

Be sensitive to what's going on in a person's life. We all have certain times during the day when we feel good and communicate more effectively and others when we just need to be left alone. If a person's body cycle is disrupted in any way, which can be attributed to anything from jetlag to lack of sleep, they make unsound decisions and act irrationally. This is not the time to ask them whether they are looking for a meaningful relationship in their life.

Where you ask is equally important. Inquiring minds want to know, but was it really necessary for you to ask him if he'd ever consider a vasectomy in the middle of a crowded elevator?

If in doubt about an answer you receive, agree. What? How can you just agree? I'm not talking about becoming someone's puppet, unless you're planning to follow in Arnold Schwarzenegger's footsteps. No, you definitely want to be your own person. But just to clarify things, simply say, "Sure, I can see your point." Invariably, this response encourages the person to elaborate on the subject. Let's say a man goes on and on about his ex-wife being such a bitch because she did this, and that, etc., etc. By simply saying, "I can see your point," they will continue on, secure in offering details. And the more details you can acquire, the better.

Cut to the Chase

I happen to favor this type of questioning as it's got me written all over it. In case you haven't noticed, I like to tell it like it is. I don't beat around the bush. My attitude is why bother? It's such a waste of time. Okay, so maybe it gets me in trouble from time to time, but for the most part it saves me a lot of time and effort. By not allowing the questionee any wiggle room, I may not get the answer I want to hear but I always get the answer I should hear. I'll take that over the latter any day of the week.

So, what do I mean by cutting to the chase? There are passive ways to ask questions, such as, "Did you see that movie?" as opposed to, "Did you like the movie?" Better yet: "Is your old girlfriend back in town?" as opposed to, "Was it fun catching up with your old girlfriend now that she's back in town?" Now which is more effective in putting their train of thought on the right track?

If you want to know if a man met an interesting woman at a party the other night, ask. You can skirt around the issue if you want, but really, if your goal is to get to the bottom things sometimes it pays to start there. Be tactful, and handle the matter with finesse. After all, you don't want to appear blunt and pushy, just direct.

REMAINING OBJECTIVE

This is most women's greatest weakness—the Achilles' heel of being one. When it comes to the opposite sex, it is surprisingly easy to lose sight of reality. The more we invest in a person, the more we like them, and the harder it is to remain clear. The truth can be hard enough to see, but even harder if we don't want to see it. Our own emotions convince us to pick the least confrontational solution to a problem, frequently blinding us to the truth. Worse, the more you like him the more likely you will be to ignore the obvious.

For instance, you are on a first date with a man who can't seem to keep his eyes focused on you for more than a minute or two. If you are attracted to him, you may dismiss this behavior as harmless, or just circumstantial. Your perception is distorted, your objectivity compromised. If his eyes consistently wander, it's a good bet that the rest of his body will eventually follow along.

Another reason women tend to look the other way is neediness. If you think you just met Mr. Right, and he turns out to be all wrong, you may latch on to him anyway. There's an old saying that goes something like the person who wants the deal the most usually gets the worst deal. The same applies to relationships. Sheer fear is what's going on here. You finally meet someone you think is it, and maybe, just maybe, there's no one else out there that's this good. Wrong! Of course there is. Don't let fear force you into making a bad decision. If you fail to act because you simply can't bear the pain of a difficult decision, remember that by not doing anything you are simply making matters worse, not better.

Do not get emotionally committed to one particular outcome. Emotional commitment can wreak havoc with your rationality. If you are dead set on things working out the way you want them to, you will ignore or distort a situation that could lead to an emotional disaster. This happens all the time when we get caught up in sex. We overlook basic flaws for the sheer pleasure of passion. Trouble is, when the heat dies down, we're usually left with a coldhearted prick.

Most lapses in objectivity occur because of delusional thinking. Stay real. Before you decide whether a person meets your needs, create a list of essential elements you look for in a mate. Put a lot of care and thought into the qualities you'd like this person to posses. Then don't hesitate to compare the live candidate to the ideal one. Convincing yourself that you can learn to love sports because he does isn't doing yourself (or him) any favors.

If making lists doesn't seem to be doing the trick, try this one. Make up some choices. If you were seeing someone else, and you met this man, would you be interested? If not, why are you now?

It's as John Wooden said, "Fear is nothing more than false evidence appearing real." The best weapon against fear is knowledge.

SNAP DECISIONS

Try not to make snap decisions unless forced to do so (i.e., a taxi driver taking a fare or a coworker related incident.)

Hundreds of pieces of information about a man will be thrown at you simultaneously. Catch as much as possible, particularly anything that stands out or seems unusual. The glaringly obvious appears as such for a reason). Gather all the information in. Then pick out five or six predominant traits and make your decision.

Let's say the hostess at a party informs you that she knows a man that can give you a ride home, focus on your concerns and identify the information you will need to evaluate him. If you suspect that he may have been drinking, check to see if his speech is slurred. Ask him a difficult question that will force him to think about the answer. If you're wondering if he is honorable, remember how he treated other women at the party.

Is he using suggestive body language? Extract the answers that are most important to you, then decide and decide quickly, or the decision may be made for you. Do not get trapped in analysis paralysis.

Bottom line: Act now, verify later.

CHAPTER EIGHT

EMOTIONAL LEAKAGE

Our outer being reflects our inner being, as most of us know. Although we may not verbalize our psychological hauntings, they become evident in our personal possessions and naturally overflow into our surroundings. Peeking into a person's office, their home, and their car (just to name a few places), gives us a broader view of their personality. You can gain access into their education, religion, marital status, political affiliations, economic status, hobbies, etc.—even if you never meet them.

It's really about using the power of observation and reasoning. The clues are easy to see; they're just sitting there. Focus and you will find the secrets of the hidden self.

ENVIRONMENTAL EVIDENCE

I was assigned to work for a new person in the office that I had never spoken to before. The day before I was to report for duty, I took a look around his office to see if I could figure out what kind of person he was.

The furniture was polished Danish modern, the artwork modern, and the files and papers organized neatly and separated into equal stacks. His degree was framed and hanging on the wall. There were pictures of his wife and two children on the bookshelf. One had been professionally taken; the other two were taken outdoors—one of the family skiing, the other hiking.

Based on this overview, I could venture to guess that his work habits were probably of an exemplary nature. He obviously wasn't a stick in the mud, as he leaned toward a contemporary decor. He cared about what other people thought, as decorative items were tasteful and chosen with care. He sought to impress. As a person I judged him to be a bit on the short side (height of his chair), athletic (family vacation photos), and in his late forties (based on the age of his children and the degree on the wall). I could also tell that he was Catholic, as there was a church flyer tossed in the trash, and that he liked vintage cars (a book on his bookshelf). The next day I was pleased to see that I was right on the mark, and prepared for it.

Also, be aware of the layout of a person's home or office. You don't have to be a Feng Shui expert to understand that a desk facing a wall is not fortuitous. Choosing this position indicates the person is closed-in. Basically, any interior design that removes barriers is significant. Is the office arranged so that you can comfortably have a conversation or so that you must sit across the desk at an angle?

Hints of who and what we are can be found everywhere. Is he flamboyant, humble, messy, trendy, neat, traditional, practical, conservative, or egotistical? Don't forget what you are looking for: patterns that will reveal a person's true behavior. For instance, if the home environment is drastically different from work, then that should be explored. Dead plants and sick animals are cause for concern. People who surround themselves with live plants, flowers, and other natural objects are generally health conscious. Messy people have messy minds. You get the idea...

Two places in a man's home that can be quite revealing are the refrigerator and his medicine cabinet. As for the fridge, don't just look at what's on the inside (nothing but a six-pack of beer will tell you enough), but also what's on the outside—magnets, photos, tickets, whatever. It can be a bulletin board of information.

A medicine chest filled with Pepto Bismol and Mylanta probably belongs to someone who is highly stressed and/or filled with hot air. Tranquilizers generally belong to those who may not be coping well. Pay attention to everything you see, and everything you don't. If he's lived in the same place for over a year and has two sticks of furniture and hasn't hung the pictures on the wall, you can safely conclude that he's either planning to move, or not wild about making commitments.

If you haven't made it to the house, you've probably made it to the car. Fortunately, how people take care of their cars is concurrent to the way they take care of their living environments (as long as the car isn't his living environment). Does it smell like french fries? Is there trash on the floor? Has it not been washed since he bought it? Yes, but what about men that are car crazy, you ask, and rightfully so. They spend hours polishing their prized possession, and you know their house isn't going to receive the same kind of care. The answer is why do you care? Do you really want to compete with four wheels and an overdrive?

Should you break up with a man because he hangs the toilet paper the wrong way? No. Evidence pertaining to the man behind the man may cause doubt or confirm what you already know. They are not deal breakers.

The most revealing props in an office: calendars; photographs (note the frames); bookshelves; bulletin boards and what's tacked on them; artwork; desk accessories, such as paperweights, pen and pencil holders, an in and out tray; workout bag; rolodex; mirrors; diplomas or plaques; and the trash can.

The most revealing props in a home: items in the refrigerator; items in the medicine cabinet; animals; collections; books; music; movies; photographs; alcohol; the garden; and indoor flowers and plants.

The most revealing props in a car: car alarm (or car club); built in car phone or car fax; music CDs; bumper stickers; seat covers and cushions; tires and wheels (particularly raised or lowered height); decorative artwork added as trim; personalized license plates and license-holder; mirror ornaments; contents of glove compartment; and what's hidden underneath the seats.

FASHION FOIBLES

"Clothes are a tool you use to control how others react to you and how they treat you."–John Malloy, *Dress for Success.*

There's no question that how a person dresses fashions the message they choose to express about themselves. The best dressed? The mall's the limit, so long as the attire flatters the wearer and is appropriate for the occasion. Sure, there may be times when one can't predict the proper apparel for every chic soiree, but that's insignificant. Purposely pooh-poohing a dress code however is not. A man who refuses to wear a tie to the office Christmas party wants to be noticed. A well adjusted person will consider their audience and dress accordingly. A meeting at a child's school will require different attire than cocktails with co-workers. Taking circumstances into consideration is just being courteous.

Wearing suggestive or revealing clothes shapes a person's perception in one of two ways: they may be overly confident or overly insecure—once again proving that self-importance and self-doubt are interchangeable. Two sides to the same coin. So, it doesn't matter which, because the bottom line is that they crave the attention.

A man dressed in what appears to be unkempt or disheveled has been hiding in a closet and knows nothing about social mainstream activities. As a matter of vogue, they remain clueless. Particularly insensitive to the protocol required at any social gathering, they would not think twice about showing up in a wrinkled (although clean) shirt, messy hair, shoes that don't match, or that look like their dog used them as a chew toy. It can also mean that they are from a lower socioeconomic background, or that they are simply stupid. *Queer Eye for the Straight Guy* may be able to rescue him, but is it worth it?

At the opposite end of the chic spectrum, we find the fastidious freak. We're talking the obsessive-compulsive type. This is the guy that doesn't have a hair on his head out of place, his shirt is ironed and his shoes shined. He can be highly structured and completely inflexible. Good luck!

A flamboyant flair usually means the person is creative, artistic, a nonconformist, independent to the point of being a bit fickle, and usually pretty imaginative. This category also includes those that alter their body in any way. If you're doing something less temporary, like applying acrylic nails, it's really not a statement of any kind. But to permanently alter your body to the extreme, whether by shaving off your eyebrows to wearing a huge, noticeable tattoo, is a sure sign of rebelliousness. It may be wise to avoid someone who looks like they would appear at the receiving end of Steven Hawking's telescope.

Conservative people care about what other people think and will dress to be accepted. These are the type of men who wear color-coordinated ties, socks, and spend a great deal of time obsessing over whether they match or not. They don't want to stick out socially and feel most comfortable adopting a practical and analytical approach to their wardrobe. They tend to squash their creativity beneath their rather conventional thinking. They are practical authoritarians who want to go with the flow and don't care if they think for themselves (although they think this is thinking for themselves). Meet the status quo.

How a person dresses can be subjective, and it takes time to tell if someone cares more about practicality than style. But for the most part, if you don't like a man's sense of style, you don't like him. Go back to the racks and choose again.

TYPES OF TOYS

Okay, as if I haven't been bad enough already, I am going to risk one more generalization. Men have Toy-dar. They buy toys. And, if they buy toys, they find other men with toys. They are drawn to toys.

Make note of any extravagances. For instance, if a man only plays golf once every couple of months, yet owns the best clubs in town, then that's saying a lot. The same can be said about the car he drives. If it's expensive and out of his range, then he's not very practical, which by the way will overflow into other areas of his life. Don't be surprised to find him wearing his Rolex to the gym and Italian loafers to walk the dog. There are hundreds of oversimplifications that can be made here, but suffice it to say that these guys suffer from low self-esteem and are extremely image conscious. They seek approval in the form of admiration from others.

SMOKE SIGNALS

Cigarette smokers have an automatic disadvantage. A prop. Whether they know it or not, the manner in which they use this prop is a dead giveaway as to how they are feeling. First of all, the act of reaching for a cigarette in and of itself indicates the need for security. It is similar to reaching for a pacifier. Also, it is often a replacement for what we would normally do with our hands. Tapping the cigarette against an ashtray is a sign of boredom. Dragging deeply is often a replacement for a physical gasp, in the manner of I can't believe that. Blowing smoke up is a sign of confidence, while blowing smoke down is a sign of distaste. Making rings in the form of a snowman's fist can be interpreted as an angry gesture.

The entire act can be used as a stalling technique, a way in which someone can collect their thoughts and strategize on their next move, without appearing transparent. Except, of course, this just makes it that much more obvious. Quit while you're ahead.

DRUGS AND ALCOHOL

Drugs and alcohol surpass all age groups and boundaries. Look for the signs—not just in someone who you suspect may be an addict but also in the occasional abuser. If you hear, "I only drink when I get together with the boys," every other day, then this person can be equally as dangerous as a serious addict. Perhaps more so.

Signs to watch for:

- Talking too slowly or too quickly.
- Red eyes, or bedroom eyes that are partially shut.
- Inconsistent behavior, especially when they lose their inhibitions. Suddenly they are talking too loudly, too softly, getting too close, getting too far away, happy one minute, sad the next. Any extreme changes in behavior from the last time you met.
- Smell of alcohol, not only from their breath but from their skin.
- Body odor in general.

CHAPTER NINE

DETECTING DECEPTION

People lie. There's no getting around that. But voices don't lie, faces don't lie, bodies don't lie. In a spontaneous fraction of micro-movement, the truth will inevitably be revealed. There's no getting around that either, even if they are not just lying to you but also to themselves.

First of all, let's discuss what deception really is. It's not necessarily an untruth. Lying is simply one form of being dishonest. Other variations of deception are intentionally omitting the truth, letting an untruth go uncorrected, or simply avoiding the truth altogether by not saying anything at all. Then there's all out fraud. Trickery is the hardest type of deception to detect because the hustler is usually adept and well-versed in the art of swindling you out or into their designs. They understand that the two most common giveaways are the voice and facial expressions, and they likely have mastered both.

The two most common ways in which we lie are by concealing information and by falsifying information. Most people prefer to conceal information rather than make something up. For one thing, it's easier to accomplish, and for another, less is at risk. If caught, the perpetrator can cover up by simply claiming to have forgotten to disclose the missing pieces.

If you don't know someone, it may take time to realize if you are being deceived or not. Initially, however, one sure way to tell if a man is genuinely interested in you or not is his level of nervousness. A smooth talker, only out for himself, is less likely to be ruffled than a man who cares about what you think. If he's trying to impress you, trying to get you to like him so he can move to the next step (which would be to ask you on a date), he's definitely going to act anxious. If he's a bit too cocky for his own good, he's probably not being genuine and completely honest.

How do you know for certain? Emotions. Emotions are what cause a person to change expressions, become nervous and agitated, fearful, or panicky. No emotions, no expressions. It's one of the reasons the polygraph test works. When emotions are aroused, physical signs ensue. Our blood pressure rises, hands become sweaty, and our respiratory rate increases.

No doubt about it: people have a tougher time telling a fib when their emotions overflow into the outcome. It adds a fly to the ointment, one that is doing the backstroke and sidestroke. Nervousness causes the mouth to dry. The result is that the person will swallow more, thereby increasing the pauses between words and sentences, both of which become excessively short or long. The inflection of their voice or the expression on their face changes noticeably. Or they simply have a slip of the tongue, as by now the lies have made it as slippery as a frog's skin, which can cause a fatal linguistic faux pas.

One of the most telltale signs of a liar is the manner in which they touch their face. Remember the old adage, "Speak no evil, hear no evil, see no evil?" Well, it's particularly true about liars, except that we may go so far as to add one more. The nose knows when something stinks. Likewise with the mouth, eyes, and ears. If he's touching his lips, chances are even he can't believe what he's saying. If he does this while you are speaking, then he's not convinced about anything you said. The same holds true for the ears and eyes. For instance, if he touches his ears, he doesn't like what he's hearing, whether it's coming out of his mouth or not.

Okay, so now you're saying, how the heck do you know if he's making a subconscious move versus scratching an itch? There's a big difference between a casual itch and subconsciously rubbing your face. Satisfying an urge is generally a quick movement, almost a brush of the area in question. But subliminally touching yourself is more deliberate and will last longer. You ask a man if he is seeing other women and he says no, but his finger immediately reaches for his eye. He scrubs the lid for a good five seconds. He's most likely lying. But before you jump through a negative hoop, wait a few minutes and see if he touches the same spot again, particularly when neither one of you is speaking. If he does, it could be a physical condition. How to be certain? Ask. Yes, simply ask him if his eye is bothering him due to an allergy, lack of sleep, whatever. If he says no, his eye is not dis-eased in any manner, then you may safely conclude that he is seeing someone else. And if not, he'd like to.

Speakers are adept at interpreting the body movements of their audience. If a number of people continuously cover their mouths during a speech, then they most likely don't believe what they hear.

During the Watergate hearings, Attorney General John Mitchell would often touch his mouth when speaking or his eyes when listening. Quite often, he would close his eyes at the end of a sentence. Likewise, President Nixon would jerk his head back, almost as if he'd been slapped, when confronted with the truth. This was obviously before witnesses were coached on how to dress, sit, act, and talk. Today, attorneys go to great lengths to repeatedly convince their clients not to touch their face while on the witness stand. Even so, if you watched the O.J. Simpson trial carefully, there were times when he closed his eyes when presented with incriminating evidence. Not a wise move.

Deceitful people wear masks. They often appear overly confident, compensating for their lack of sincerity. Their expressions are generally fake, their smiles forced, tight-lipped, and overly asymmetrical. Pay particular attention to the length of the expression. Any that are prolonged (anything over the five-second mark) are being forced and most often faked.

Smiles are the easiest of all expressions to fake. They take the least amount of motion and muscles. As we learned earlier, real smiles originate around the eyes. If the smile is genuine, the eyes will crinkle and sparkle. Seeing white on both sides of the pupil is normal, but seeing white on the bottom is not. There's hostility and anger brewing if you see three white areas instead of two. Ogle the ogre. If he doesn't look back with those evil eyes, that's even more portentous. Those who lie can't face the other person. Unless of course, they are well-versed on the subject of dubious deliveries, in which case they go to the opposite end of the spectrum and stare too hard and too long. If someone speaks the truth, they won't have a hard time gazing at someone and then glancing away at normal intervals.

Men that con women have mastered the art of the eyes. When asked by the police why they were so taken in by their assailant, the majority of women responded with a comment about the man's eyes. The words, "It's the way he looked at me . . . how he looked me right in the eye and melted my heart," are typical examples of men who swept their victim right off her feet and away from her money.

On the other hand, pathological liars have a tendency towards excessive blinking. It's a nervous habit, which is almost always psychological, not unlike wringing the hands together. This means they are not only uncomfortable but also bordering on angry. If they keep touching themselves, especially in a patting motion, then they are trying to reassure themselves. They are either lacking confidence in what they are saying or are highly insecure.

At times when people are placed in a position where they are on the spot and cannot move freely, such as an interview, or when being chosen for jury duty, they often give themselves away with hand movements. Instead of shrugging their shoulders, they will use the hand shrug. The what? The hand shrug. When a person is trying to promote their own seemingly helpless start, openly soliciting a person's approval, they will rotate the hands, thereby exposing the palms. Believe it or not, in the majority of cases, we tend to believe that a person is being more open and genuine when they facilitate the use of such hand-some gestures. As may be suspected, those who try to take advantage of another will also take advantage of this seemingly harmless body movement.

Some liars will touch others in a hard manner, i.e., a crushing handshake, as a means of asserting control. Beware of one more thing—one of the most common by the way—amongst those trying to pull the wool over your eyes. After years of studying how people behaved when telling the truth versus an untruth, psychologists discovered that those who were lying made more errors in their speech and would frequently go back over their sentences to correct grammar usage or poor structure. This often causes them to clear their throat or stammer. They also noted that a person's body movements generally slowed to match the rate of their speech. They most often talked less and more slowly.

Men will often loosen their tie immediately after telling an untruth. Not to mention the fact that sticking a finger under their collar might make you wonder if things aren't getting a little hot under there. If the shirt fits correctly, so will your assumption. If they gesticulate like a mad Italian, then suddenly stop, well, mama mia something is not right in the land of the boot. At this point, they might even place their hands in their pocket or hide them from your view. This is a good time to remember that it's hard to gesture when you're trying to think about what you are going to say next. That's because trying to talk yourself out of a jam is not the easiest thing in the world to do. If you're listening carefully, it's guaranteed you'll hear them give themselves away. The conversation will almost always be peppered with "ums" and "ers" (they hesitate in an effort to come up with what to say next). Similarly, the tone of their voice will rise an octave. Most people have a higher-pitched voice when they tell a lie. More proof that they are thinking too hard. Honesty doesn't take that much effort.

The content of their conversation is equally as important. Beware of people who continually bring you gossip about others. The majority of those that tattle with tales are two-faced and generally searching for information from you (which, by the way, they will ultimately use against you). If questioned about a statement they made which isn't true, they will often go off on a tangent to explain themselves. They will give you far more information than you ever asked for. If not, they clam up completely.

It's easier to lie to someone over the telephone. All you have to go by are the words, the tone of voice, and perhaps any unusual pauses. Manipulating any of these is simple sight unseen. If you are making an important decision, do not do so based on a phone call. There is no substitute for a face-to-face interaction.

PLEASE, MISLEAD ME . . .

Misleading a person may seem innocent, but it is still dishonest. Unfortunately, it happens most frequently in a romantic setting. Shakespeare attested to it in his sonnet:

"When my love swears that she is made of truth,
I do believe her, though I know she lies;
That she might think me some untutor'd youth,
Unlearned in the world's false subtleties.
Thus vainly thinking that she thinks me young,
Although she knows my days are past the best,
Simply I credit her false-speaking tongue;
On both sides thus is simple truth supprest,
But wherefore says she not she is unjust?
And wherefore say not I that I am old?
O, love's best habit is in seeming trust,
And age in love loves not to have years told:
Therefore I lie with her, and she with me,
And in our faults by lies we flatter'd be."

Here the lie is viewed as positive. It feels good; therefore, it must be good. What a bunch of B.S. that is. Essentially, this is running games between two people who want something. She wants him for her own designs, and he wants her because she fulfills his self-serving needs. No harm done. This is a benign act. Well, not necessarily. What if he believes she is going to marry him one day, and she has no intention of doing so? Is this lying? Yes. Fraud is fraud, and certainly the most harmful of deceptions. If both parties do not agree, someone always ends up getting hurt in the end. Or in Shakespeare's case, ends up dead.

WHY PEOPLE LIE

Men lie for a lot of reasons. Some do it for a living (i.e., used car salesmen, lawyers, politicians, etc.) and find it necessary for survival, even under oath in a court of law. Some do it because they can't do anything else. And some do it because they can't help themselves. They actually start with a lie and word backwards. These are pathological liars who simply don't know how to deal with the truth. We'll never know why they lied, because they don't know why they lied. That's a complicated area that few of us will encounter, and if we did, we would not have a hard time detecting it. Generally, in these cases it will not take a detective, or a psychiatrist, to uncover the truth and help us pack our bags. Unless of course you've been carrying some of that luggage around for a few decades, in which case you should unload them along with the man.

During hard times, I took several jobs in law firms. Talk about meeting master manipulators. Anyway, that's another book. But one attorney I worked with, although single, routinely wore a wedding band during court appearances. He said he thought the jurors would find him more "credible." His attitude was, "What can it hurt?" Well, for one thing, I personally never believed a word that came out of his mouth.

What can be difficult to detect are people who lie occasionally, usually out of sheer malice. The real motive lies in the need to keep up a positive self-image. Said image is likely apocryphal in the first place. Therefore, the truth poses a threat of some kind. So, out of sheer self-preservation they will first skirt the issue and then if that doesn't work, rape it completely.

Even nice people lie sometimes, probably to avoid a loss of some sort. They don't want to throw away whatever it is that's on the line.

And let's not forget the obvious. Some people like to lie. It gives them a sense of superiority when they actually pull one over on another person. Adrenaline rushes through their anemic veins, shooting them up with satisfaction and smugness, especially if they've managed to deceive a person of authority in their lives. They are addicts.

GO FOR ORDER

Fact versus fabrication. Here's the thing to read into this: if someone tells you a true story, then the sequence of scenes can be scrutinized. If taken out of order and/or deleted and added at random, you should stand to be corrected. If the tale is made up, chances are the author won't fix the faults, as he probably can't recall the exact plot line verbatim. And, if he makes the mistake of attempting to piece together his narrative with misinformation, or a completely different story altogether (which believe it or not happens), then the prose becomes poisonous. The mouth becomes the stalactite.

An amateur con man will have his story down to the last preposition. He's memorized the details to the point that he can tell the story backwards, forwards, and upside down. What do you do then? No one is that perfect. Most men make a few mistakes. There's a big difference, however, if he tells you he opened his business in June, when the last time you asked the answer was December.

Here's an example from the book, *Telling Lies,* by Paul Ekman. He sites a case wherein James Phelan, an investigative reporter, describes how McGraw-Hill and others were conned into buying a biography of Howard Hughes. People were stunned that Clifford Irving could accomplish such an impossibility from a recluse like Hughes. But that he did. To the tune of $750,000 and another $250,000 paid to him by *Life* magazine to publish three excerpts. How did Irving get away with such a hoax?

"He was a great con man, one of the best. Here's an example. When we cross-examined him, trying to break down his story, he never made the mistake of telling his story the same way each time. There would be little discrepancies in it, and when we'd catch him up, he'd freely admit them. The average con man will have his story down letter-perfect, so he can tell it over and over without deviation. An honest man usually makes little mistakes, particularly in relating a long, complex story like Cliff's. Cliff was smart enough to know this, and gave a superb impersonation of an honest man. When we'd catch him up on something that looked incriminating, he'd freely say, 'Gee, that makes it look bad for me, doesn't it? But that's the way it happened.' He conveyed the picture of being candid, even to his own detriment—while he was turning lie after lie after lie."

I THINK, I BELIEVE, I KNOW

Psychotherapist Carl Jung was once asked if he believed in God. His response was, "I do not need to believe, I know."

I know holds the highest conviction. If a person knows, then they are not sanctioning subjectivity. It's been proven to them, and they need not question their decision further. They know. Jung stated that he had more faith in his own experience and, for him, simply believing wasn't enough.

That's because if someone believes in something, they leave room for doubt. They are saying that they have a connection, but no commitment, to the decision. Their words remain biased. "I believe he came home at two in the morning," leaves plenty of room for reservation.

I think, doesn't mean much of anything. It's too wishy-washy to hold credence. If a friend says, "I think he's a nice guy," what does that mean? He's a nice guy to them. Maybe. It not only allows for the fact that they may be wrong but also that they based the remark entirely on personal prejudices. It expresses weakness. "I think I can sell this for less," means they probably won't.

OVER EXPLAINING

If someone goes to great lengths to explain to you how they never lie, then I would bet you an entire month's salary that they do. And not only do they lie but they may also think they're good at it.

The need to elucidate eradicates the statement entirely. Anyone that tells you they aren't racist, usually is racist. The bottom line is this: If someone has to account for their positive attributes in any area, then they probably don't exist. Explaining how great you are usually means you're not. It's a lie.

Actions speak louder than words. End of story.

QUESTIONING THE LIAR

Most liars are pretty clever. However, it takes a real pro to anticipate all the questions that may be involved in his deceit, and hopefully he's missed a few. Ask if they are lying, you ask? Well, yeah. You have to be careful, though. Posing questions point blank won't do you any good (too obvious, too easily avoidable). There's another way to approach this. You must ask without asking.

Let's say a man breaks a date with you because he claims he had to drive out of town on a last minute business trip. You know it's the, "You wouldn't want me to lose my job, now would you?" stuff. So, you do what any good girl would do and Map Quest the man. Later, say something like, "Wow, I heard about that accident on the 101. It must have been horrific, the way they described that ten-car pile up right by where you would have exited. It must have taken you hours to get there."

Is this lying or misleading someone? Good question. Yes and no. I prefer to think of it as creative questioning. In case this strikes you as hypocritical, bring up something less lethal. Ask about the weather in that particular city on that particular day. If you say, "Gee, it was pouring there, wasn't it?" you'll immediately know if he was telling the truth about going or not, simply by the way he reacts. "Raining, oh, ah, err, yeah, raining. It was awful. I forgot to even bring an umbrella." Think he was really there? I don't think so.

It's important that you learn how to ask the question to get its optimum effect as well. Don't give a man a way out. "Do you know if Sandy has been in town lately?" is one way to find out if he bumped into his ex-girlfriend or not. However, an evasive answer is likely. Asking, "I heard Sandy was in town, is that true?" is much more specific, and eliminates ambiguity. "Do you know about her past?" won't get you as far as, "Tell me about her past." Imply that they know the answer already, which would take a lot of effort for them to get around. You don't want to give them permission not to respond.

Why ask, "Did you get into a car accident?" instead of, "How did you get into that accident?" Remember, the three rules that all good fisherman live by: Presentation, presentation, and presentation.

Another way to finger a fibber is to offer a similar situation and see how they react. If you and the man you are seeing have recently decided it's time to make the relationship exclusive, but lately you suspect that he's not holding up to his end of the bargain, bring up a comparable case scenario. "Gee, my girlfriend is really upset. Her boyfriend just told her that she was the one and that he only wanted to be with her forever. But when she called him last night, she couldn't find him. Then he finally answered his cell phone at two in the morning and when he heard her voice, he hung up. I think he's seeing other people. I just don't know what to tell her to make her feel better."

If the man offers advice, then he's probably not following suit. But, if he starts to fidget and otherwise become uncomfortable, there's something amiss. He may well be on the heels of the boyfriend's footsteps, and this is all falling too close to home. You'll be able to tell immediately just by paying attention to his reaction. If he repeats the question, he's thinking about how to react (truthful people don't need to think), likewise if he repeats the question back to you, which is just another method of stalling. So is asking, "What do you mean?" He knows what you mean.

Sometimes they'll get close to telling the truth, with statements such as, "That's all I have to say on the subject," because anymore would be a dead giveaway that he's hiding something. The same applies to remarks such as, "I wish I could tell you more, but . . . " or, "I'll tell you this much," because they do not wish to elaborate. Beware of convoluted answers and overly impressive evasions.

Occasionally, a person will protest to a particular question. You would think that they might realize this would send up a red flag, but they don't honestly believe this to be the case. They prefer to look at it as a control mechanism. I say give it right back to them. If they refuse to answer, you refuse to respond. I don't mean to freeze them out with a cold shoulder, but do remain silent. During an extended gap, the participants in the conversation become uncomfortable. Allow it to get to that stage, where tension has built because neither one of you is saying anything. The trick? Do not fill the space. Instead, remain your normal, charming, pleasant self. I guarantee you he will cave faster than an air conditioner salesman in Alaska. At first he freezes, then he spills his guts. This can be quite informative.

What do you do if he still says nothing? Then he is probably trying to hide something, especially if it would involve denying an accusation. This form of unresponsiveness is usually associated with deception. He may also be playing games, wanting you to feel jealous or insecure. Men often do this to keep you off guard and control you. All of these are possible motives. Still, if you examine them closely, they are all excuses for suspicious behavior.

In general, people who have nothing to hide are happy to answer any question. You should be even more concerned if the person you are questioning is normally communicative. To be certain, you might try asking the question again at a later time.

Another method con artists employ is mirroring. I talk about mirroring in a positive way later on, but it can also be used to deceive. In this case, they are generally mirroring your feelings toward the object of their desire. For instance, they may volunteer to take your necklace, which seems to have conveniently broken, to be repaired. You express concern over the cost. They agree and reiterate how expensive the necklace is then suggest it wouldn't be a good idea. They have taken on your reaction to your own property. They may even tell you a story about an expensive item that was entrusted to someone and then not returned. You sympathize. Again, he offers to take the necklace to the jewelers, except this time his emotional elixir clouds your judgment and you agree. Trust me—you will never see your necklace again.

Exaggeration is another way in which a lie is covered up. Let's say a man is cheating on his wife and speaking to his lover on the phone. She enters the room and asks, "Who was that on the phone?" He is caught. He panics, and his face is now red and his hand is shaking as he hangs up. He looks at his wife and says, "It's my mistress of course! She's calling to find out where I am. She thinks maybe I am cheating on her."

Who was on the phone? His mistress, of course. Did his wife pursue the issue further? No. In this case, stating the truth did not require mental abilities, merely coolness under pressure. If it ever happened again, the wife should ask to speak to the mistress. See what happens then.

One last point about liars: If they lie to you once, they will almost always do it again. During police interrogations, criminals are "tested." If a suspected rapist claimed that he was charged for a minor sexual crime when he was ten years old and it turns out he was twenty at the time, then that's a big lie. Anything else he says will be subject to scrutiny, including the fact that he committed the crime.

I knew a woman who dated a man I used to date. They were quite serious, to the point of actually moving in together. I knew this man quite well, well enough to know that he lied about his age. He told everyone, including employers, that he had been born two years earlier than he actually was. I'm not sure how he accomplished this on his driver's license; however, I was pretty much done with the guy and didn't care. Still, I was appalled to discover that the girl he was about to marry didn't know his real age. It might have had something to do with the fact that she was a lot younger; however . . . I have to stop there. How would you ever believe anything this man said beyond that—let alone plan on spending your life with him? I wished them well and moved on. They got married. It lasted two years.

RECALLING OR REMAKING

The truth is all in the eyes. Another rabid superstition? Hardly. During a typical conversation, we are either remembering an event that already occurred, or constructing something new from scratch. As we put our thoughts in order, we are either doing one or the other. How can this be used to tell if someone is lying? Whether we realize it or not, our eyes move in one direction when we recall and another when we remake. Pretty darn consistently. You can rely on it.

So, the first thing you have to do is establish which way their eyes move when they are recalling a past event, as opposed to figuring out what to tell you about it. Police officers use this technique often. They will establish a rapport by keeping the conversation light and relaxed. Not only are they getting the other person comfortable but also collecting thousands of bits of information to determine whether the suspect may or may not be lying.

Start by talking about something they have no reason to lie about but that you know would require some thought, some conscious effort of digging through those dusty old file cabinets in our mind. Ask the person what it was like growing up in whatever town they grew up in. Or ask them what color their mother's eyes are. You can also use less personal information such as determining the last time they took a vacation and inquiring about local sites. Anything to do with where they've been and what they've done are usually an honest recollection.

If they say, "Let me think about it," then they are definitely trying to recall information. If they say, "I wonder what it would be like . . . " then you know they are constructing a situation. Next, ask an intangible question, such as, if they could own any car they wanted to, which one would it be? What color would it be?

Once you've established whether they are recalling, or recounting, notice which direction their eyes break in. Information pulled from our memory is generally factual, and therefore, you can assume it to be the truth. Whereas, fabricating facts require a person to create ideas, words and statements.

There's one exception to this rule, and that is if the person has committed the lie to memory. I have a friend who has been lying about getting a college degree for so long, that when asked he absolutely looks and acts like he's telling the truth. He's lied about it so often that it's become truth. His truth.

As a rule, most people look down and to the left when they lie.

THE LYING RAT

There are many kinds of rats, but the particular species I want to dissect is the most common, and the most devious. This rat lures you in and then gets you hooked. Often for no particular reason than to see if he can. It's definitely an ego booster on his part—someone he hunts for the sport. In pursuit of building up his already inflated ego, he will feed you so much of his drug that you can't help but become addicted.

How does he accomplish this? Well, it pretty much works the way it does with all rats. Real rats. Scientists discovered that if you place cheese at the end of a maze consistently, the subject, although rather enamored by the convenience, loses interest. However, if the cheese is placed at the end of the maze sporadically, the subject will go for it every time. Why? Ambiguity is addictive. The most common way the rat plays this game is to lead a woman on. He is a chronic flirt. He uses all kinds of tactics to manipulate his prey. You have to give him credit, for he's usually quite adept at understanding body language and its effect on women. He will lean into you when you are talking and tilt his head ever so slightly to show genuine, fake interest. He will lick his lips at every chance he gets (in anticipation of the two of yours meeting his). He will touch you often and with great affection. He leads the woman though, and once she suggests they get a bit closer, wham! He backs off. Then he comes on again. The stop, go, off, on, I love, hate you, need you, don't need you, has her hooked big time, and he can prove to the world, and himself, that he's attractive physically and sexually. At this point, he can basically get whatever it is he wants from her.

Unfortunately, in a relationship, addiction often turns to obsession. Then you're doomed. The fixation keeps you from living your own life. Somehow or another, you begin to believe that you aren't anything without this man, and if he's unresponsive and inattentive, so much the better. This heightens the stakes, increasing the ante. *Ah, if only he would love me, my life would be so much better.* You spend so much time (wasted time) wondering that you can't possibly have time for creativity, friendship, and fun. And call him? Oh, heaven's no. That would give you clarity, which would increase the possibility of getting unstuck. Obsession is almost always just another form of procrastination. You don't have time.

If this type of animal tries to weasel his way into your life, do not let him. The longer you hang around, the harder it will be to ditch this egotistical, highly insecure loser with commitment issues.

HOW TO TELL IF A MAN IS HIDING SOMETHING

Being secretive is not a positive trait in a man. If a man is hiding something, you need to know what it is, or at least why. One of the most telltale signs that a man is keeping secrets is that he will instinctively and routinely cover or remove any personal material from your view. He will whisper a lot more frequently, especially when having telephone conversations or conversations with anyone else. One way to notice if it's intentional is to see if his posture changes at the same time. If a man is hiding something while on the phone, he will have a tendency to hunch over more, into a guarding position, or if face-to-face with a person, they will turn away partially.

People hiding something are more apt to look around the room when being addressed, rather than returning a gaze. Or they look down during a conversation. In addition, if they cover their mouth with their hand more than they ever have before, then there's something they don't want to tell you. Even if their mouth isn't covered, which can become obvious, their lips will remain tightly closed, the jaw set.

Secretive people will keep their personal lives to themselves, keeping their distance from anyone that might get too close. It's almost as if they are afraid that you'll see the real person. A person they do not like.

Key Behaviors to Watch for:

- Looks down and to the left
- Touches their face by placing their hand over their mouth, tugging on their ears, scratching the nose, rubbing the eyes, etc
- Perspiring
- Blushing
- Voice tremors (or any other change in the voice, such as rapid speech)
- Gulping, throat clearing, stammering, stuttering (when they don't normally do any of these)
- Shaking

- Fidgeting with objects, i.e., playing with their glasses, tapping a pen on a desk or notepad, playing with the buttons on their shirt collar
- Will turn their body at an angle away from you, usually toward the closest exit
- Creates a physical barrier if possible; will step behind a desk or move to the other side of a counter
- Any signs of nervousness such as clearing the throat or coughing nervously, smiling nervously and running the tongue over the teeth, putting their hands in their pockets, eyes darting, body tensing, shifting in his seat

Key Phrases to Listen For:

- You may not believe this, but . . .
- To be honest . . .
- Do I look like I would do something like that?
- Honestly, I have no reason to lie to you.
- I swear . . . (And be particularly wary if they are swearing on something, such as the Bible, their mother's grave, or anything else sacrilegious or sacred.)
- I have no reason to lie to you (quite often means that they do).
- I don't remember, I can't recall, or not that I can think of. (Although some people have trouble remembering, most won't use these phrases excessively in a conversation unless they are purposely trying not to.)
- I can't recall. (On Watergate tapes, Nixon was continually advised to answer serious allegations this way. He was repeatedly coached to answer with, "I just don't recall.")
- To the best of my recollection. (Lawyers love this one, as it gives their client an easy out in case they are guilty.)

SIGNS OF NERVOUSNESS

Most people don't like lying. It makes them uncomfortable, and in an effort to defer said distress, some signs of nervousness seep out through the skin. At the beginning of a lie, the person may appear quite calm. They are not shaking, or tapping, or shifting weight. But if pressed, the poison becomes toxic and the body screams for an outlet. Sure indications of illegal doses of a panic attack are:

- Wringing their hands
- Chewing nails
- Looking away or down
- Excessive clearing of the throat
- Rocking in their chair
- Eyes darting back and forth
- Tensing the body
- Fiddling with anything they can get their hands on
- Shifting weight from side to side
- Becoming quiet

HOW TO TELL IF A MAN IS CHEATING ON YOU

For some reason, men lie abut other women the most. Whether they are married to you or not, committed to you or not, they simply will not fess up. Usually, it's because they want their cake and the ability to eat it, too. Could be he's a womanizer, who simply finds the opposite sex irresistible. In this case seduction is first and foremost on their mind. Or, it could be a woman throws herself at him, and he gives in faster than a brassy blond at a convention

Well, we're not going to quote Jimmy Carter on the subject of lust, but suffice it to say that contemplating cheating is fine, acting upon those lascivious impulses is not. The reasons why he strayed are really irrelevant. For once you think you're the one, only to find out that you're one of many, it hurts like hell. Using the techniques above to find out if he's lying are all recommended, but along with that here are seven signs that he's cheating:

1. He won't tell you exactly where he is, or when he will be back.
2. He dresses up to play poker with the boys.
3. He takes, and makes, mysterious phone calls.
4. He smells like another woman (and not his mother).
5. He changes his regular schedule for no apparent reason.
6. He forgets he made plans with you, and then can't remember the details.
7. He is no longer interested in having sex with you.

The best key to unlocking a liar? Inconsistency. That's right. When a man lies, his words won't match his expressions, or his actions. They may say they love you more than life itself, but if he crinkles his nose with disgust, and crosses his arms over his chest, then chances are he has closed up his heart and isn't going to open it up again until something changes. And that would be him, not you.

CHAPTER TEN

SIGNALS THAT CAN SAVE YOUR LIFE

It took me a long time to learn that just because a man is nice does not make him a good person. Being nice is a conscious decision, not a character trait. "He seemed like such a nice man," has gotten so many women in so much trouble. Why? Because it's how the majority of those with sinister intentions steal their way into our homes, our cars, our jobs, our beds, our life, and our life insurance. Often this is merely a man's intro into your world. He will do anything to ingratiate himself and make you feel obligated.

One key characteristic he will look for is your ability to be manipulated. If you say no, you have to mean it. Changing your mind about one thing only lets him know that he can change your mind about anything. For example, if you have an old flame calling you fifty times a day, and finally, out of sheer exasperation, you answer the phone, basically what you've conveyed to this person is the fact that if they call fifty times, you will pick up. So, you'll get on the phone and demand that they not call you again. Guess what? They will. I guarantee it. When you say no, mean it.

The same holds true on a date. Playing hard to get is a dangerous game. It doesn't make you more desirable; it makes you more of a sucker. Once you've gone back on a no, they know. No matter what you say, they are in control because they can always change your mind.

Many men have been taught through their culture, movies, and advertising that a woman says less than they mean. They often interpret no to mean maybe. Therefore they keep trying, which makes the game that much more desirable. Winning is everything. It's up to you to make them hear more than what is being said. Saying no and not meaning it is perpetuating a lie—the lie that this is how people in love are supposed to act. Never mind that your brothers, fathers, cousins, and other men demonstrated their love by pursuing a woman endlessly, with or without her consent. After all, the woman is encouraging them, right? This is basically a load of crap. It only works in B movies—not in real life.

Another way in which men attempt to gain the upper hand is to insult you in some manner. Typecasting is typical. He may say something such as, "A girl like you would never talk to someone like me." Or, they may take the opposite approach and place themselves in the same boat as you. They will compare whatever problem you have to one of their own. "I'm having a hard time with this project, too." Or, "I noticed you're carrying a Weight Watcher's cookbook. I've been trying to lose weight for forever." And, to further ingratiate himself, he offers too many details about how this has become an issue in his life, right down to his mother who was obese or a sister who tried to get him to go on the cabbage soup diet.

A word of warning about a man that comes on stronger than King Kong. Do not monkey around. Be straight and to the point when you explain that he cannot determine that you were destined to be together for all eternity in a matter of minutes. By mapping out your entire life for you, he will only succeed in getting you lost. Premature promises command attention because they are a ploy to command your life.

Red light signals should flash if anyone goes out of their way to research you. You just met; however, he's taken it upon himself to call your best friend (mother, sister, whomever he happened to meet early on in your relationship). This may be appropriate if they gave him the impression that he could take such liberties, and if he's asking them what type of food you like or your favorite color. This is unacceptable if he demands to know where you are every Monday night when he can't reach you. Being hypersensitive to your needs, to the point where you feel that you and you alone are responsible for his happiness, is not only dysfunctional but damned irritating. Who wants to be in charge of someone else's happiness?

Would you willingly drive your car into oncoming traffic? Would you willingly light the fuse on a stick of dynamite? Would you walk across a minefield without knowing where the mines were? The answer is obviously no. But then why is it that I see women jogging in the park with earphones on? Why do women choose to walk down a dark alley, instead of taking the longer route around the block? Or if they must take a risk, why do they not opt for the middle of the street? Why do teenagers fall for such lines as, "You look more like a woman than a teenager," or "You're a grownup, and you can come with me if you want," and then get in the car with a total stranger? I could go on and on.

Please, avoid danger at all costs. If you are in doubt, better to be safe than sorry. If the elevator door opens up to a seven foot man, balder than a bomb, who says, "Hey come on in, girlie, name's Curly." Do not get in. Repeat: do not get in. If you fear someone is following you on the street, coming at you from behind and speeding up the closer they get, immediately cross the street, if possible, so you can see who is behind you. Walk fast, but do not run. Head towards other people. Take out your cell phone and call the police, informing them of your exact whereabouts.

Remember, muggers and molesters are on the prowl for an easy target—someone that won't call attention to them. Someone easy. It's your job to make attacking you more trouble than it's worth. Do not walk with your head down and your shoulders slumped. If coming face-to-face with a potential conflict, stand firm, looking your perpetrator directly in the eye. Do not smile. Do not engage in idle conversation, thinking you might make a friend out of the man that might kill you. While remaining aggressively confident, make yourself appear taller, stronger. If seated, stand up. If in a closed off area, place a barrier between you and the assailant, such as a chair, a table—a wall would be nice.

When I was single, my mother always told me to keep an old pair of my dad's shoes by the front door. I didn't quite get it, until the phone man showed up to make some repairs. He spooked me. But the minute he stepped inside he asked how long I had been married.

"Not long," I replied, adding a quick, "He's sleeping, so do you mind keeping it down?" I still kept the front door open, while holding my cell phone at all times. I also paid particular attention to the repairman's actions. Did he go straight to his job, asking few questions that are only work-related while maintaining a comfortable distance? Did he touch any of my personal possessions and peek into areas he had no business peeking into? He didn't. But if he did, I would not have hesitated to ask him to either reframe, or leave.

No one wakes up one day and says, "Gee, I think I'll be psychotic today." That's why, if you are paying attention, the signs and signals are there. Heed their warnings.

<u>At the outset, be wary of a stranger if</u>:

- He's trying to buddy up with you in one way or another, even if it's uncalled for. Nice people won't approach you unnecessarily. If he is interested in a "pick up," he'll try to make a date, not try to move in.
- He is over-complimentary, or overly insulting.
- He offers unsolicited information about himself.
- He tries to talk you out of whatever you said no to.

<u>Later, be wary of a stranger if</u>:

- He is verbally abusive (to anyone, including waiters, the car valet, anyone…).
- He resolves conflicts with violence.
- He breaks things on purpose.
- He uses money to try and control you.
- He happened to be violently abused as a child.
- He acts overly jealous.

<u>What to do if you are Threatened</u>

First of all, figure out if you are in immediate danger? If so, do whatever it takes to get out of it. CALL THE POLICE! Otherwise, it's the person being threatened who decides exactly how powerful that threat will be—not the person doing the threatening.

Fear is the bargaining chip they use to gamble on a favorable result. Act scared and they've won the game. Be nice and you'll give them an excuse to come back for more. Bear in mind that their threat is a last resort. They've tried everything else and have succumbed to a "do this, or I'll do that" mentality. Actually, it's a good sign. They're trying to intimidate you by causing mental anguish, which is by far better than physical anguish.

If the latter were the case, there would be no negotiation. Trust me on that. "You'd better do this or else," or, "until you come back to me, I won't stop calling," are the types of threats they need to get you to do what they want. If you're not clear about what exactly that might be, ask. That's right, ask what it is they want from you and why.

Then what? Don't do it. Don't even talk to them about not doing it. Repeat: do not engage them in any manner whatsoever. Stop contact. Often times, you are a drug that they are addicted to, and you must detoxify them as quickly as possible. Otherwise, the drug, you, consumes them faster than rat poison. And we know all about rats, especially the lying kind.

But wait a minute. Tell them you won't do it? Yup. That's right. Unless of course it causes harm to you or someone you know and love. In which case, we go back to the beginning. CALL THE POLICE! Otherwise, if they threaten to tell your husband that you slept with them, are sleeping with them, or whatever until you give them an outrageous amount of cash, then offer to put your husband on the phone. In most cases, you won't hear from the man again. Granted, this oversimplifies a myriad of potentially harmful situations. However, the upshot remains the same. If you do not take the bait, they have no choice but to back off.

If you hear words like if, or else, unless, until, then the culprit only seeks to cause uncertainty toward his own gain. Handle it on your terms, not theirs.

Should you get a Restraining Order?

Whether you should obtain a restraining order is strictly an individual decision. One that cannot, nor should not, be made for you. Essentially, however, consider whether or not the man would respond negatively towards the court order by becoming even angrier.

In the movie, *Enough,* the character Jennifer Lopez plays arrives at the police station beaten and bruised and asks the officer what steps she could take for a "friend." He brings up a restraining order. This response was far from encouraging. She wanted to know if she should throw it at him the next time he tried to attack her. Sad as it seems, she was right not to pursue the matter. A court order would only have made him that much more violent.

Remember this: 75% of all spousal related murders happen after the woman leaves.

CHAPTER ELEVEN

HOW TO ATTRACT THE RIGHT TYPE OF MAN

"Mingled with these groups were three or four match-making mamas, appearing to be wholly absorbed by the conversation in which they were taking part, but failing not from time to time to cast an anxious sidelong glance upon their daughters, who, remembering the maternal injunction to make the best use of their youth, had already commenced incipient flirtations in the mislaying of scarves, putting on of gloves, setting down cups, and so forth; slight matters apparently, but which maybe turned to surprisingly good account by expert practitioners." --From *The Pickwick Papers* by Charles Dickens.

I have a really sweet girlfriend. A good person. And, at times, I just can't stand her. She enters a room and suddenly a wave of men swells up out of nowhere. Not only that, she will leave with at least a few phone numbers and a promise of, "You bet I'll give you a call." Meanwhile, I've spent half the evening trying to get up the courage to speak to one man, only to discover that he left. With someone else.

How does my nameless friend do it? She's not drop dead gorgeous (which is the reason she remains nameless). I mean, she's cute, with a nice figure, and she dresses with style, while managing to accentuate the latter.

And she's no dummy. But that's not it. You can ask the men, and they'll tell you they don't know—that there's just something different about her. Imagine specks of light flying out from her flesh like airy bubbles, sticking to the transparent skin of the eye. They see it. They just don't know what it is.

She does. Because when it comes to attracting the opposite sex, my girlfriend possesses an attribute more powerful than looks or brains. She has an irresistible fundamental command of body language, which she uses to her full advantage. From the minute she enters a room, she signals her message in a kind of Morse code of motions. "I love being a woman, and I am available." Then when she sees someone that genuinely interests her, the message changes to, "Wow, I am attracted to you, and I'd like to get to know you better. Do you feel the same way, too?"

The process itself is undetectable, as the metamorphosis appears effortless. For to try too hard, as with most artistic endeavors, would invariably kill the concept. Watching her, I discovered that she understood how to communicate without saying one word. That which was not, is.

It starts with the walk, one that would make any man's head turn. The way she carries herself speaks of breeding and sensuality without being obvious. It's kind of a sophisticated, toned down Marilyn Monroe walk. She stands with her hips slightly forward and rolls them when she turns. Her posture is always open and relaxed, one hand usually on her hip. If the person she addresses closes up, with their arms folded, she will fold hers, wait a minute, and then unfold them, invariably convincing him to do the same. If a man's mouth is tightly drawn, she will smile and continue to do so. She stands close enough but not close enough to appear invasive. She touches people gently and, if receptive, often. She laughs about everything. And she makes direct eye contact with everyone she faces. Her focus remains directed at one person at a time, in its entirety, making that person feel special and appreciated.

But mostly there's a shine in her eyes that really can't be described or taught. What is it that puts it there? For one thing, this is a woman who is not afraid to be sensual. A woman who is not afraid to be relished and enjoyed. She loves to be loved.

How can we learn her techniques? Let's start by entering into her world.

<u>Come On In</u>

You're out at a party. You'd like to meet a man. What do you do? First of all, you position yourself advantageously. Don't hide. It might sound obvious but people do it, especially if they stay in the same spot for too long, which is just another form of remaining hidden. Mingle, mingle, mingle. Then find a good place to stop once in a while. The two best places to plant yourself in a home are in the kitchen or by the bathroom. At a party, hang around the edges of the room where you are more accessible, or by the food. What better excuse for someone to saunter over to your side? Sooner or later, you're bound to see everyone.

If you are seated, make sure there's room for another person to sit beside you. Men do this all the time on airplanes. They put their coat or briefcase on the seat beside them. The minute they spot an attractive woman, they move the object. If he's standing and you are sitting, and there's no way for him to join you, then you should stand up as well. If one of you is standing and the other sitting, both of you will feel uncomfortable and intimidated by the difference in height.

According to a study by the Social Issues Research Centre in Oxford, UK, 55% of a first impression is based upon a person's appearance and body language. You want to give the right impression by being open to any advances. Do not hold your glass, or anything for that matter, directly in front of you. Do not fold your arms. Do not lean against anything. Try not to sit with your legs or ankles crossed. Do not clutch anything, such as the arm of a chair, your knee, or a pillow. These all give you the appearance of trying to, quite literally, get a grip.

Once you've made eye contact, it's important to capture his attention. Lock eyes with him for a second, then smile a Mona Lisa smile. What makes the picture so attractive is that flirtatious smile she wears, while glancing at her prospect sideways. You catch his eye, then what? Look down and away. Then, wait one brief second before slowly bringing your eyes back to his. This time hold his gaze a little longer than socially acceptable (approximately four seconds), smile, and now you can continue with whatever it was you were doing, or pretending to do, before you were so delightfully distracted. If your eyes remain locked too long, one of you will become embarrassed and look away permanently.

Wait a few minutes, and check back with him. By chance you catch his eyes again, smile a warm, friendly smile. Keep it up. You want to make him feel secure enough to come over and talk to you. Hopefully he will smile back. At this point, you should feel a connection of some sort—a slight tingling of anticipation, passionfruit flavored Jell-O in the knees, or something similar. Otherwise, why bother?

Movement attracts attention, so if he doesn't look back right away, get on the move. If your back is toward him, place your hands in the back pockets of your pants. If you are seated, cross and uncross your legs. You can keep your legs crossed and still show signs of interest. How? Dangle your shoe off the end of your foot. It's a way of saying that you like him, and that you feel comfortable around him. Then try to move into an open posture, as he'll be less inclined to believe he'll be rejected and that you won't bite him if he comes over.

When he does, check to see if he is in an open position. Is his drink held to the side, hands relaxed, not clenching anything or stuffed in his pockets, and arms extended in a relaxed manner? However, if he hooks his thumbs in his pocket or his belt, he's hooked on you. Thumbs pointing downward, especially toward his crotch, is always a good sign. His feet should be slightly apart and firmly planted on the ground, not resting on the side of the toes. If the stance is too overt (i.e., hips thrusting forward), trust me, he believes he's God's gift to women.

If he's sitting, he should have one leg crossed over the other with an ankle resting on one knee and/or have both feet flat on the floor, similar to Abe Lincoln in the Lincoln Memorial. Does he straighten his tie or adjust another piece of clothing? Smooth back his hair? All good signs. If per chance his eyebrows rise a little and his facial muscles relax to the point where his jaw drops a bit, then he is still not sure. Smile your biggest, winning smile and that should take care of any residual resistance on his part.

What do you do when he finally comes over? (And you wait for him to come to you, please.) Once he introduces himself, shake his hand. That's right. Shake his hand. First of all, it's a great way to touch him, and if your intuition is up to speed, combined with your expert knowledge of handshakes, this gesture alone can offer vital information. And I have to tell you right now, there's no bigger turnoff than a girlie girl handshake. Those Scarlet O'Hara, give him your fingertips and tilt your head so he can kiss your hand days are long gone. Likewise, if you offer both your hands to him at once. (If you do this at all, only do it with another woman, and only if you are trying to console her). The only impression that this gives a man is that you are submissive. If you are, then why are you reading this book?

Keep your handshakes firm and solid. Offer your hand from a straightforward position, squeeze firmly, and release. If a man tries to offer his hand palm down, then he's already trying to dominate you. Beware. You want a gentleman. One who shakes your hand like an equal, without being forceful, and who smiles at the same time. Anything short of that usually belongs to game players and little boys.

Now that you are face-to-face, you both size each other up, whether you admit it or not. This is just an outward, do you like what you see kind of thing. Generally, however, we evaluate people on the basis of three crucial criteria. First and foremost is how they look—their physical attraction, whether they are taller or shorter than you suspected, fatter, thinner? How old does he appear to be? Secondly, whether their voice resonates with ours. Is it too deep, too squeaky? Does he have bad breath? Thirdly, the way a person smells plays a crucial role in our romances. It's later that we'll actually want to know things, like what he does for a living, where he lives, and his cultural background.

Let's say all three check out a-okay. Should you proceed? Well, it all depends on whether or not he's interested. Notice how much he looks at you. Michael Arglye, in his book *The Psychology of Interpersonal Behavior,* noted that people that look at each other sixty or more percent of the time are fascinated in the person, more so than what they are saying.

Without realizing it, he begins matching your posture. He may sit or stand in the same position as you. If you are sitting on a couch, one leg crossed over the other, you may find that after a couple of minutes, he is sitting in the exact same position. Pay close attention, however. These are signs that he's interested, as he's definitely mirroring you, but if he's holding his knee or ankle, or pinching himself in any way, he's also insecure and needs to relax a bit more.

He licks his lips, and his eyes are sparkling. He reaches over and "accidentally" touches you on the arm or back. He lowers his drink and begins caressing the top of the glass. Or puts it down altogether and flashes his palm during a hand gesture. (Showing the palm of the hand is a sign of openness and honesty.) He takes off anything—a jacket, a tie (hopefully not the rest of his clothes quite yet).

The most obvious suggestions of rejection are moving the body away, tilting the head forward, yawning, folding their arms, and looking at the ceiling. When a man turns his body in a forty-five degree angle away from you, he means thanks, but no thanks. Tapping his fingers or a foot, swinging a leg, looking at his watch, blank stares, and holding his head up in his hands are also signs of indifference.

If he keeps looking at other women, there's not a chance in hell you want to be with this guy. Even if he's not looking at other women, and still looking away, he's not interested. If he makes a move to brush anything off his clothing, such as lint (real or imagined), he's subconsciously trying to give you the brush off as well.

Open up the conversation and see if he steeples his fingers (a disguised steeple is when they use the index fingers of each hand and positions the tip of the steeple on their mouth instead of under their chin) or puts his hands on the back of his head, or if he examines his cuticles. All signs of arrogance. Other patronizing gestures are excessive compliments, fatherly pats on the hand or back, and peering up over his glass at you. Indications of overconfidence are also not desirable. If he's too slick and too smooth, let him slip away.

If he's interested and you're not, then move on. A word of warning here. Studies indicate that men are more receptive to inviting behaviors than rejection (i.e., yawning, looking at the ceiling, checking your watch, checking out other men). Men most often misread these signals and will continue to make advances. What can I say? Not much. But I can tell *you* what to say. When all else fails, and signals are crossing faster than Dennis Rodman, speak the truth. "Thanks, but I'm not interested" should do the trick. If it doesn't, please leave. Without the man.

What if everything is copasetic? The two of you are actually hitting it off. You're interested and based on your knowledge of body language, he concurs. Let him know. Look him in the eye. Adjust your clothing (i.e., pull down your sweater, realign your lapel, take off your jacket, put on your jacket . . . you get the idea). Keep your shoulders back and stand or sit straight. Lift your hair up from your shoulders, as if you are hot. Be brief and not too obvious—you just want to give him a peek of your neck. Touch your necklace, if you are indeed wearing one. Face toward him, and tilt your head slightly when he speaks. Don't hurry or be pushy. Take your time now, as confident people do not appear overly excited or anxious.

Keep the initial dialogue brief. At this point in time, your desire should be to determine if you are physically compatible and any future possibilities exist. You will gain much more ground if you don't appear as if he must ask you out. Once he does, or you do, then cut the meeting short. You have to go; you're busy. Keep him guessing, and get the heck out of there.

Now you can go to the next step because even though you haven't said but a few words to each other, except maybe, "Hi, how are you?" your bodies have spoken volumes. This is the most difficult obstacle to cross: initial contact. If you've gotten this far, you're home free.

Just one more thing, which may sound stupid, but do it for me, pretty please. Make sure he's single and available. You do not want to proceed beyond this point if he is not.

SURE SIGNS OF SEXUAL INTEREST

- Exaggerated smile or exaggerated laughter
- Primping, touching their hair or touching you
- Winking, blinking
- Wetting the lips or rubbing the tongue over the lips
- Thrusting out the chest or hips
- Invading your space and trying to isolate you
- Crossing and uncrossing legs repeatedly
- Giving a person the once over by examining them from head to toe

---

Sit Right Down

You've reached the point where you are ready for the next step. You are officially on a date, which I believe is where two people get together and pretend that they are people who they are not, so the other person will find them worthy enough to go on another date with the person they are pretending to be.

Pick the best environment where you can create a comfort level, so the conversation can thrive and blossom. I have a friend who takes all the women he meets to a Moroccan restaurant, where you sit on the floor in a private area. The meal is served over seven courses and takes approximately two hours. Some people like this and some don't. How does my friend know? He asks, as should you especially if you take the lead.

Exercising control has advantages. Then the meeting should be on your terms. Have you ever noticed that when a boss delivers good news he comes to your office, but when it's bad news, he ends up inviting you to his? Not an accident by any means. There's a trade off going on. Information for domination. On your turf, the other person will be more guarded. On his, he will be more likely to open up and confide in you.

Where you position yourself is extremely important. To make someone feel most at ease, make sure that their back is toward the wall. People tend to be more open when they are not in a closed environment. Ideally, they should face the center of the room, and be seated by a window. Sitting side by side, or at an odd angle, is generally not a good idea. It's hard to have a conversation and, since the relationship is probably quite new, both of you will probably feel awkward. Remove a large bouquet in the center of the table that you can't see across.

If you're in a home, or office, remove potential obstacles. Have you noticed that speakers often move away from a podium when giving a speech? When being interviewed, a potential employer will not likely leave his desk, unless he is interviewing someone on the same level. By removing potential "blocks," they appear more receptive, which will automatically make you more receptive.

TURN OFF YOUR CELL PHONE. Any distraction can be fatal to a meaningful conversation. Your words should flow like a river. They may twist, they may turn, but they can't do a nosedive over a cliff and turn into a waterfall. Any distraction is a potential liability.

Also, you can test someone's interest now by nodding your head and watching to see if they mirror your movements. Surreptitiously, place your hand under your chin. (I talk about mirroring and exactly how to do this in a later chapter.) As the saying goes, imitation is the sincerest form of flattery, and if he follows suit, it's a definite sign of interest. This person likes you.

Now is the time to pay attention to details that you couldn't possibly have noticed during your initial meeting. For instance, take note of his interaction with other people. Lawyers can't possibly get to know possible jurors, so they observe their actions carefully. They draw a lot of conclusions based on their body language and their interaction to other people and to them. If possible, try to see how the man reacts to people at a party, especially a work related event such as a company retreat or cocktail party. You'll be amazed at how much you can find out in no time at all. Is he mingling with superiors, co-workers? Is he treating his subordinates equally? How closely does he approach the person he is talking with? Does he dominate the conversation? Does he flirt? Notice how he addresses the waiter.

My girlfriend insisted that I meet her new love interest. This guy got quite a build up. Not only was he the handsomest, most intelligent man in the whole world but according to her downright nice. You can imagine how shocked I was when I finally met him, only to see how much he had her fooled. She gave new meaning to the term, love is blind. In her case it was not only blind, but deaf and dumb. Her boyfriend wasn't particularly friendly to me, but I let that slide when it became apparent that he'd expected me to bring a date and not show up solo. Then he drove like a maniac, cursing at someone that cut him off in traffic. He practically pushed the valet out of the way after handing him the keys to his car. He was rude to the waiter, finally sending his meal back, and didn't leave much of a tip because, "Why should I, after the service I received?" It took a while for my girlfriend to realize the guy was a jerk, but thank God she did.

Basically, he treated people as if they weren't there. This is most prevalent with snobs dealing with any kind of "help" that they feel they don't have to treat as equals. I have witnessed doctors talking about me as if I weren't in the room and have had bosses call me to their homes to pick up something they obviously thought was a matter of life or death, only to have them greet me at the door in their pajamas without even the slightest hint of embarrassment or apology. It doesn't matter what status you have in the world, it still doesn't give you the right to treat people in this manner. Those that do are only interested in one thing—themselves.

A truly thoughtful, confident man treats everyone in the same manner. It shouldn't matter if he's conversing with a grocery store clerk or the president of a company. Nor do they change how they react to someone depending on their own personal mood. People are creatures of habit and develop a certain method in which they deal with life's challenges. If they are not treating other people well, how do you think they will treat you once the fire dims and you're dealing with daily disputes?

My mother told me never to consider marrying a man until you have traveled with him, seen him sick, and made him untangle the Christmas tree lights. Again, not bad advice.

Walk With Me, Talk With Me

Is it love at first sight? Usually it's not what we say that makes our hearts go giddy-up. When you first meet someone, anyone, talking about our inner feelings can be difficult and, at a first meeting, inappropriate. The conversation can be quite uncomfortable at times. Here are a few points to help you over the hump.

People feel extremely comfortable when they hear their name. Strangers don't call strangers by their name. (This is one of the reasons I hope you don't let your children advertise their name, be it on clothing or otherwise. When a stranger calls someone by their first name, it commands their attention. They feel they must know this person.)

Start and end conversations on a positive note. There's an old adage that goes, "If you can't say something nice, don't say anything at all." Of course, this is unrealistic in the long term, but it's definitely something to keep in mind in the early stages of a relationship. This is not the time to point out every mispronounced word. Aside from the fact that this exposes your own insecurities, it is a sure fire way to clam up the conversation. Whatever you do, resist the urge to call attention to a man's mistakes, or worse criticize him for them. I think you're being a bit hard on yourself, will take you a lot further than, I can't believe you did something that stupid.

In general, men only hear half of what you say anyway. I mean that in a nice way, but it's true. So when you say, *don't forget to take the trash out,* all a man hears is *forget to take the trash out,* and believe me, he will stay true to the words, too. Especially if there was a pause between the *don't* and what you didn't want. Instead, say, "I really would appreciate it if you took the trash out later today."

This can also work to your advantage. *Don't fall in love with me,* might just make someone fall after all. In the words of Dwight D. Eisenhower: "Leadership is the art of getting someone else to do something you want done because he wants to do it."

Talk about yourself, but more importantly talk about what you like to do, what interests you the most. You're trying to set it up so that there's a reason for a second date. Ask what he does in his spare time, what his hobbies are. That way if there's no mention of getting together again, you can always ask a question that alludes to a topic he brought up earlier. "Since you love cars so much, and I am buying a new one, perhaps you can help me out?" Asking for favors, or help with something, is a great way to set a second date. (Be reasonable, and do not suggest he paint your garage.)

Be careful not to reveal too much, and this goes for your attire as well. Men love secrets. They need a certain amount of mystery. Otherwise, there's no reason to continue with the chase. Unless, of course, they're looking for a causal relationship or seeking another accessory for their arm. Men looking for a trophy girlfriend don't care how interesting you are, as long as you look good. In this case, you will look even better with someone else.

Look him in the eye when he talks to you. Nothing will make a person feel as if you are paying attention to them, and enjoying what they are saying, more than that one tiny little movement. Here's another point I learned the hard way: people like people who listen, but attractive people talk more. Try to talk and listen in equal proportions.

Nod your approval of what they are saying, or in some cases, nod a couple of times to let them know they are on the right track and that they should continue. You're interested. You like what they have to say. Lean back to offer openness but forward when they are speaking of a subject that they find particularly important to them.

You can be expressive with your hands; however, do not get carried away. It's easy to start throwing your hands about over dramatically when you are nervous or on the spot. The only thing I accomplish by doing this is knocking a drink over. So, do use your hands, it's a good sign, but not to excess and not to the point where you are showing your palms too frequently. This is a sign that you are trying to convince someone of something rather than being sure of it yourself.

This is going to sound very Pollyanna, but I have to tell you right now that I personally never had a problem with the chick. I mean, really, here's this girl that walks into a whole city full of mean, cynical people and decides, hey, let's just take a positive approach. Take a lesson. Keep your chin up. Literally, keep it up at all times, even if you don't feel that way inside. If nothing else, it eliminates a double chin.

Touch him often. Everyone likes to be touched, especially by someone they like. You can increase or decrease the amount to suit his comfort level. But if he likes it, do it and do it often, just be appropriate about it. Touch his arm, or place your hand on his when you want to get his attention. Reach over and feel the fabric of his shirt, or examine a tie tack, cufflinks, or any other accessory. On purpose, accidentally bump into him. This way he's getting used to you touching him without even realizing it. As the relationship progresses, this will make it much easier to be intimate.

Be confident. Men and women are attracted to a person who won't compromise their values and beliefs. Confident people maintain an even keel. They don't get overly upset, overly anxious, overly nervous, or overly excited. Make it appear to be a given that you can walk away at any time. It's not necessary for you to chase him, as you don't need him one way or another. Give him the impression that you are definitely interested, but if it doesn't work out, or if you happen to change your mind, oh well. You're outta there. Adios, amigos.

Ask the right questions. Shake some old bones until they fall out of the closet. Keep alert, listen long, and watch closely until you turn their very flesh inside out. Therein lies the essence of their being. And, if you do not find it, you will not walk away empty-handed. Live and learn. You become that much stronger.

I Think I Found My True Love

How do you know that you've finally found Mr. Perfect? You don't. You will have to get to know him better before you can determine that. But one thing you can tell right off the bat and that is if he has the makings of a man who is mentally healthy and happy. Leaders come in all shapes and sizes, but what makes them most attractive is their mental atmosphere. Following are seven signs of a successful person that I personally hope you look for and find in a man:

1. They say what they mean and mean what they say. In other words, they are consistently conscious of their words and actions, and they take responsibility for them.
2. Typically, they will attract quite a few people. They have many acquaintances and a substantial number of good friends. (If you

are somebody's only friend, perhaps you should think about why.)

3. They willingly volunteer for things most people wouldn't dream of volunteering for. Although unpleasant, they still don't mind helping out.

4. They rarely invade another person's space. They have no need to prove themselves, like most control freaks.

5. They face the person they are speaking with directly, making good eye contact, titling their heads to signal that they are listening carefully and interested in what the other person has to say. Sitting or standing, they will lean forward, nod, and offer at no emotional cost, a few words of agreement to encourage the recipient to continue with the conversation. They will keep their hands off of their face and never cross their arms in front of their chest. People in positions of power rarely steeple their fingers.

6. They are good looking, even if they aren't attractive. Because they are conscious of their appearance, they maintain healthy habits, physically as well as mentally. They have an erect posture and a confident stride. They pay attention to how they dress, taking care that it is appropriate for the occasion. Whatever they choose will generally be tasteful and conservative.

7. Last, but definitely not least, they smile a lot. A big, genuine smile that attests to the fact that they love life with its many adventures and surprises that can literally stir their souls

This mate is the type of man we should all seek. Two people should come together in any relationship to bring out the best in each other. If not, what's the point?

CHAPTER TWELVE

SPEAKING A MAN'S LANGUAGE

What makes a man fall in love with a woman? Well, wouldn't we all like to know? After all, we're talking about a mind far superior in complex connections than the computer that tracks the Space Shuttle. At first, we might guess that a man would say something concerning a woman's physical attributes. As the saying goes, "Men fall in love through their eyes, women through their ears." Ergo it must be the way her long, golden hair fell over tanned shoulders like a sparkling waterfall. Or, perhaps the way her body moved in the slinky blue dress that made her look like a long, cool drink? Or, maybe it was just her big boobs. Initially, this may be true. Physical attraction is a powerful enticement. Sexual attraction is even more powerful. But, as most of us know (or should know), neither lasts long. Aphrodisiacs fade faster than cheap perfume, and if the foundation falters because of the absence of solid ground, you can kiss him goodbye.

So what's the "something more?" Ah, good question. Now, I'm by no means an expert on men, but I am a pseudo-expert on women (being one myself) who has been left, dumped, ignored, and blown off. Call me crazy, but I think men want the same thing a woman wants. Understanding. If someone understands you, really connects with you, then you can let down your guard and be yourself. And if you can be yourself with someone, then you feel safe, secure, and comfortable. You trust them. And if you trust them, you will automatically fall in love with them. Real love. Deep, true love. Because they are not falling in love with an image of you. But you. Now that's powerful stuff.

So, how do you understand a man? Okay, let's rephrase that. How do you understand a man and love him anyway? Well, before you toss this book in the trash, allow me to explain.

Psychologists have discovered that people perceive the majority of their world through one of their three major senses: sight, sound, and touch (feeling). Taste and smell play a significant role, but predominantly we use one of the major distillates to communicate our ideas, our moods, and our thoughts in a consistent and congruent manner. Most people make the mistake of continually packaging information by using the sense they navigate on, as opposed to the one the person they are trying to convince uses.

It is no surprise that advertising is mostly visual, as visual people comprise the majority of the population. Discovering why a man reacts the way he does is like discovering a road map to his mind. You will instantly be aware of what irritates him and, likewise, pleases him.

Have you ever said to yourself, "He's just not listening to me," or "He's not seeing this my way at all," or "If he could only understand what I'm going through right now." Sound familiar? Chances are you weren't tuned in to that particular person's wavelength. You simply weren't making sense to their particular senses.

Next time the opportunity arises, watch a successful salesperson in action. Chances are they mastered the art of interpreting, and then speaking, a potential customer's language. They ask pointed questions directed at determining which approach to use to successfully close a deal. I'll give you a couple of examples. Say a salesperson is trying to sell you a new suit. He might start out by asking, "What do you see yourself in?" He receives no response, other than a, "Well, I don't know . . . um, err . . . " The salesperson has now determined that his client is not visual. His next question would probably be something along the line of, "How does navy blue sound to you?" If there's still no response, he may ask, "How does this fabric feel to you?" Bingo. The client begins touching the fabric and rubbing it on his skin. Ah hah, he is kinesthetic (feeling). The salesperson has acquired the tool necessary to deposit convincing clues into the subconscious mind. He concentrates on the feel of the fabric. The way it fits and moves upon his patron. It works with everything, and it is much more effective than just taking a random stab in the dark when it comes to getting someone to see the light.

Let's say a woman wants to convince her husband that they need a new washing machine. She knows (because she's read this book) that her husband is auditory. Instead of telling him how much better it would work, or how much cleaner the clothes would be, she could explain that the newer models are so quiet he would barely hear them.

Eyes can be used to determine what language a man speaks. Visual people will look upward when talking, auditory people look from side to side, and kinesthetic people look down. This is a much more reliable method of determining which plane a person uses to communicate and interpret information. For instance, a person could say, "I don't see how that could happen, it just doesn't sound right to me." Are they visual or auditory? If this is a relatively short conversation, check their eyes. The eyes move more rapidly than words ever will. In fact, they rarely stay still.

Also, determine if they are speaking figuratively or literally. If someone says, "Boy, I hear that," and they are speaking to you on the phone, that doesn't make them auditory. They hear you because they can't see you. Likewise, if a person is describing a picture they tend to apply visual language to their thoughts. If they are recounting an experience, they will generally relate to feeling words. Remember, literal specifications can change with the circumstances, whereas figurative meanings usually do not. When discussing a future event, there's no reason to say, "I'd like to see that happen," unless you're a predominately visual person.

Can a person change planes of communication? Yes, of course they can. None of us are that cut and dry. Most people can shift from one to the other with ease, under the right circumstances. The situation, the mood, and circumstances can affect how a person responds. A quiet, kinesthetic person still gets angry. If you happen to catch him at a moment when he is particularly passionate about a subject, you may assume he is auditory.

All of our senses are important to us, but we will always rely consistently upon one more than another. The point is, we can shift or swerve from time to time, but we tend to understand everything in terms of our own type. Visual and auditory often overlap, and everyone moves to the kinesthetic plane once in awhile. Sooner or later, we all have to feel what we're going through. It's human nature. But establishing which navigational tool a man prefers is essential to influencing him.

This can be used to your advantage, even in the bedroom. Some men will prefer to look and then touch (visual). Some prefer to snuggle first (feeling). And some insist upon talking your ear off before they do anything at all (auditory). Mastering his mind will make you completely irreplaceable to him. Why? Because he can talk to you in a way he can't talk to anyone else. Maybe even be a bit vulnerable. How cool is that?

It could take weeks to explain all of the nuances involved in each type of "language." However, here are some basics that will help you determine the true personality of a man—and the most effective way to interact with him.

THE VISUAL MAN

Visual people comprise the majority of the population (approximately 60%), and because of this they are also the easiest type to spot (no pun intended). For one thing, they are always looking around. Their eyes dart here and there, trying to get the whole picture. Often their eyes jump upward when responding to a question, as they are trying to "see" the answer. If someone brings up the past, he'll recall a picture. Likewise with the future. He'll visualize the outcome in his head.

Generally, he dresses well. Still, he'll be certain to ask you how you think he looks. He worries about his age and whether it shows. He'll wonder how old you think he looks, even if he asked you that question yesterday. He combs his hair a lot. This is the type of guy who won't be caught dead, not looking good. Running to the grocery store, may require time to take a shower and change clothes.

His house looks good as well, and not just well decorated but well organized. Just try and rearrange the books on the bookshelf and see what happens. Pictures in the home are also important, usually picked with care and hung with precision. If you haven't guessed by now, a visual man can be a bit of a perfectionist. Not to worry, just don't mess with his things too much, even when he's thrown them about helter-skelter. There's method to the madness. They'll pick it up and organize it sooner or later. (Don't be surprised if you find out that the card you bought him for his birthday is in the trash, as they are not usually prone to hanging on to the past.)

Loud music and lots of talking make them feel uncomfortable. They don't like to talk about their own feelings. It takes awhile for visual men to share. If they have a problem, they generally brood, rather than spilling their guts. (Not a pretty sight.) So, how do you get inside their head? You might try asking how they picture the situation, and he might be more open to discussing it. Visual people respond better to yes and no answers because it's easier to pin them down. Get straight to the facts.

Not only are they constantly searching around to see how things look, but they'll also talk about subjects in the same manner. How does the project look? They prefer seeing the results, usually quite quickly. They are often high-energy, workaholics. And with all that flitting around, they have a tendency to breathe quickly. If you want to get a point across, write it down. They would rather read than talk any day. Usually visual men know what they are doing and where they are going. In fact, you will probably find a lot of maps in their car. They watch other driver's like a hawk.

Film director Francis Ford Coppola is obviously a visual man. Instinctively, he views the world through his eyes. To demonstrate what I'm talking about, I read somewhere that he was driving in his car one day and wanted to dictate some notes. But he didn't have his tape recorder with him and a notepad was out of the question. So the story goes that he produced an imaginary tape recorder. In his mind's eye, he loaded it with fresh tape, pushed the button, and began to speak. He listed each item as if he really had the mechanism with him. Later on, when he sat down to recall his taped message, he didn't have a problem. He activated the whole list just by rewinding the tape. Now that's a visual man!

If you are having problems communicating, do not demand that a visual man tell you how he is feeling. They freeze up. What you want to do first is to get them to visualize the overall picture. Then you can really talk. You almost have to see his feelings with him.

Picturing a visual way of thinking is the key to what motivates this man. Appeal to his ego and flatter him. Tell him how handsome he looks when he says he loves you and he'll say it all the time. It's that easy. Do you see why?

How to Impress the Visual Man

This may sound rather old fashioned for an independent woman of the twenty-first century, but one sure way to impress a visual man is to dress the way he likes you to dress. Before you go off on a tantrum and burn this book, think about this. The last time you went to a party, or any other special occasion with your best friend, didn't you call to find out how to dress? It wasn't because you wanted to please your friend; you wanted to fit in and to be dressed in a manner people attending would appreciate. So, why not do it for a man?

And don't assume he wants you to look like a sex kitten, wearing short skirts, tight sweaters, and sexy lingerie, either. Every man is different, and what appeals to this man may not be so stereotypical. That's why it's important to find out what he likes visually. Perhaps a preppy look, or more of a bohemian look, turns him on. Chances are it's basically your style anyway, or he wouldn't have been attracted to you in the first place. All I am suggesting is that you emphasize the positive.

It goes without saying that appearances are of utmost importance to the visual man. He will notice your hair, whether you had your nails done or not, your clothes—especially if you are wearing the same thing you wore the last time you went out. He's not going to expect you to jump out of bed looking like a model, but he will not tolerate you looking sloppy for an extended period of time. Running around the house with curlers in your hair, a green facial mask slopped all over your face, or wearing an old bathrobe that's so worn in places you can see right through it will not impress him. Try to look the way he likes you to look, and again, I mean that with the best of intentions. If he mentions that he likes you in red, wear it. Find out which body part is turning him on the most, and try to accentuate it, especially in public. If he loves your legs, it's always a good idea to wear skirts.

He will also get "hooked" on a certain expression when you are happy to be with him. You can make him feel good just by giving him that look, whenever and wherever you please. Unfortunately, he'll pay more attention to the expression on your face than the words coming out of your mouth. So, if you wish to shed a different light on things for him, you should use words that prompt him to see your side of the story. If your goal is to go to a movie, don't say a movie tonight sounds good. But rather say it looks good. (By the way, pick a movie with lots of action. Chick flicks are not his cup of tea.) Don't say, "I understand how you feel," but rather, "I can see how you feel that way."

The visual man needs a lot of time to look things over before you approach him. He doesn't want to make a decision on a sales pitch based on what he's heard. He's going to want to see the proposal and read it first.

In that respect, you cannot jump all over him. He wants you to look first. Since he likes to look, there's a bit of the voyeur in him, and since they are always up for a show, nothing turns them on faster. And that's all I'm going to say on the subject.

He even prefers food that looks good and will be less likely to taste something if it appears to have been regurgitated. Always keep his favorite movies on hand. He's the type that can remember every movie he's ever seen, and not only that but he also knows who starred in it, what year it was made, the best scene, and the worst scene. Coffee table books, magazines, and anything else he likes to look at will be invaluable. Whatever he tells you he sees as being his kind of thing is important. Make a mental note of it.

Visual Triggers:

A picture of the two of you together is a great trigger. Every time he sees it, it will have an impact on him, so will anything else he can look at that will remind him of how much he loves having you in his life. Buy the flowers that he bought you for the very first time and make sure you have them in the house whenever he visits. Eat in the restaurant where he said he loved the view. Write him notes and hide them. Sticking a note in his shoe that says, "I love you heart and sole," may likely send him over the edge. Mail him love letters and cards about things he enjoys or finds funny.

Key characteristics:

- Outgoing, generally not shy
- Makes a decision quickly and effortlessly
- Likes to talk but wants to see the results

Key careers:

- Anything to do with the arts, such as a director, cameraman, editor, photographer, graphic artist
- Pilot
- Designer: interior, landscape, clothing
- Advertising

- Publishing
- Architect

Key phrases to use:

- Do you see what I mean?
- I'm in the dark about that.
- It looks good to me, how does it look to you?
- Are you starting to get the picture?
- What's your point of view?
- It's easy to see the writing on the wall.

Key environment:

- Clutter free, neat and tidy (including smell)
- Light and airy, and any place with a gorgeous view

Key activities:

- Taking pictures
- Sightseeing
- People watching
- Watching the sunset
- Theater
- Often prone to collecting things, especially beautiful or rare things

THE AUDITORY MAN

There are two types of auditory men—one that hates to talk and one that can't shut up. The first is simply not interested in talking to anyone else because he's too busy talking to himself. He has a lot of conversations with himself about his life and his problems and analyzing both, then coming to a decision, and reanalyzing that decision. It's safe to say that any interruption could be a potential problem.

The other type likes to fill in all of the silences. That means that if he's not talking and no one is talking to him, you can bet that he'll turn on the television or the stereo for background sound. Rarely will you find him in a silent room, by himself, even if he's asleep.

Either way, auditory men like to talk when they want to talk. When they buy something new, they shop around forever, discussing the item endlessly to anyone that will listen before finalizing the purchase. It's less likely that you'll see him running around wanting to look at the merchandise first (like the visual man) because he'd rather listen to a sales pitch over the phone.

What he sees and feels are important, but ultimately what gets his attention is what he hears. He truly cares about what you have to say and loves to have long conversations about almost anything. The right words, spoken in the right tone of voice, will stimulate his feeling; otherwise, it's hard to get him to open up. Part of the problem is that he's already had long discussions about his problem in his head before he'll even get around to discussing it with you.

Unfortunately, that can cause a blow up when you least expect it. Good news is that they are not prone to screaming and yelling. If this happens, tell him that you'd really like to hear the solution that sounds best to him. He's very analytical, after all, and loves looking for an answer. If that doesn't work, call him on the phone. An auditory man responds well to long telephone conversations. Or opt for a quiet evening at home, just talking. He can read your feelings by the tone of your voice. His advice will be practical and calm, even if you're not.

Remember, not a sound will escape him. So, not only is he adept at listening to what you say but also to what you don't say. Choose your words carefully, as he won't forget them. Auditory men have a tendency to be extremely logical, and they will organize their thoughts, as well as their possessions. Although, an auditory man is less rigid than a visual man and will generally not put things back in their proper place. The absent-minded professor loses (pardon, misplaces) a lot of things. That could include you.

If his eyes dart from side to side when you ask him a question, you've definitely peaked his interest. Keep talking. If he tells you something interesting, ask him how he heard about it. In general, ask what he thinks, not what he feels. And, of course, be all ears.

How to Impress an Auditory Man

Okay, right now, learn this. You can spend hours making yourself look gorgeous and this guy will barely blink. This is not the type who notices that you just spent four hours in the beauty salon getting a completely different hairdo. You're going to get all excited and blurt out, "Well, what do you think?" And he'll say, "Did you say something?" He may not always see what you see because he's not that interested in the visual. If you're expecting him to notice that you spent hours cleaning the house and making this fabulous looking meal with candlelight, etc., he's not likely to go gaga on you. Not that he won't appreciate the effort; he just doesn't always know how to show it.

If you want to impress him, make the right sounds. What's really turning him on is the fact that you have his favorite music playing on the stereo. If he loves the ocean, make sure he can hear it. Or if it's the sound of birds and nature, find some, even if you have to take him outside. Suddenly, you'll see him relax and become himself. Trust me, it will be worth it.

Another place that seriously requires the right sound is the bedroom. He can't get enough of you telling him just how good he makes you feel. When you say something that makes him happy, stick with it. The words not only have to be familiar, but consistent. Talking in his rhythm is important. Never be loud when he's not. It's very distressing to him.

If he's not responding to you, don't touch him. He doesn't like to be touched first. He has to instigate affection, and you should let him. Basically, what you have to do is to talk him into it. In fact, you have to talk him into almost everything you want or need. Showing him won't do it. Touching him in the most loving manner possible won't do it. Hearing it will. If you want to remind him to do something, such as a doctor's appointment or whatever, do not write it down. He will lose it. Tell him about it and remind him verbally.

Suggest events that require sound—a concert or a musical. If you really want to be creative, leave loving messages on his voice mail at work, on his cell phone, and at home. He loves to hear you talk, especially if it's about him.

<u>Auditory Triggers</u>

If you want to have an "our song," this is the guy for you. When a song hits a special chord with him, be extra loving. He will associate one with the other for the rest of his days.

Finding words that are special for him, or making them special for him, are essential. I had a girlfriend who was dating an auditory man who didn't want to be intimate because he was overweight. He'd never been hefty before, and his self-confidence was shot. He tried to lose weight, but didn't. And she wasn't willing to wait. So, she made up a game when they were together. Rubbing her hands over his chest, she whispered how much she enjoyed playing in the forest and, moving further down, how much she loved visiting the cabin where Mr. Winkie lived. All she had to do after that was tell him that she couldn't wait to knock on the cabin door, and he was ready. It may sound kind of silly, but anything does if you're not one of the people in the situation. Make up your own story to tell. He'll love it.

Special nicknames can be highly effective. A woman, who is being intimate with an auditory man, simply has to whisper a special name in his ear at the right moment and he'll always associate the two. It doesn't have to be silly either. It's more the manner in which you say it. For instance, if his name is Scott and at a crucial moment you lean over and call him Scottie in a sweet, sexy voice, he'll place the feeling he's having with that name. Anywhere, anytime, you say Scottie in that same manner will bring him back to that exact same place. Listen, it works.

<u>Key characteristics:</u>

- Not really extroverted, but not introverted
- More likely to be willing to listen
- Not in a hurry to make decisions, but will put them off
- Prefers facts to theories

<u>Key careers:</u>

- Musician
- Radio Personality
- Writer
- Lawyer

- Salesperson
- Public Speaker

Key words to use:

- I hear exactly what you are saying.
- That sounds right to me.
- It rings true.
- You are preaching to the choir.
- There's a little voice inside of me telling me that this is right.

Key environment:

- Pleasant sounding, around waterfalls, or quiet countryside
- Usually have some kind of background sound (television, music)

THE FEELING MAN

The feeling man judges the world and everything in it by how he experiences it. Kinesthetic is what he is, if you want to get fancy. I don't, so let's move on. Well, you'd think that this guy would be easy to understand, especially since the shirt he's wearing, which won't be trendy because he doesn't really care how he looks, has his heart embroidered on the sleeve. Because they are extremely intuitive and generally motivated by their gut feelings, they can be highly unpredictable, somewhat spontaneous, and frequently fickle. A lot of inexplicable reactions to things are explained away with an, "I don't know why I did that; something just told me to do it." Even if they don't particularly like someone, the reason may be shrugged off with, "I just get a bad feeling about him." Not only is their love blind but so is their hatred. Their relationships will definitely not be logical.

Obviously, they won't hide their emotions. They won't be afraid to cry or express their feelings openly and honestly. Here's the trick, though. They allow their feelings to show in order to illicit a reaction. If they are sad, you simply cannot ignore them. They want your comfort, your sympathy. If they are unhappy, they need you to snap them out of it. Or at least try. The good news is that they reciprocate if and when the tables are turned. Feeling

152

men care about how you feel about things and will worry if they think they upset you in any way.

Physical comfort is essential. You'll notice that if they can get away with it, they opt to dress informally. Even their car will be purchased with comfort and practicality foremost in mind, rather than the way it looks or the way they look in it (like a visual man). Basically, things should feel good. They melt between soft, satin sheets. They like to touch a lot and be touched in return. One of the nicest things you can do for the feeling man is to give him a massage. Give him one often, and you'll have him wrapped around your well-oiled finger in no time at all.

Yes, they cry openly. But that doesn't mean they are wimpy. A wimp is a different story. So, just because they get quiet, and start looking down at the ground a lot, doesn't make them pushovers. They are assessing and reassessing their feelings about the situation. And don't stare. They sense that you are looking at them. They breathe slowly and deeply. These guys have a whole dictionary full of sighs, which it would pay to learn to translate next time they sit around being mellow (which this homebody prefers to any other activity).

They definitely like to hang out. They want to be close and enjoy snuggling. The feeling man is extremely uncomfortable if you travel without him. They will eat a lot, or drink a lot, or over indulge in anything that makes them feel good, until you're back in their arms again. These loveable slobs, who can't seem to get their socks to match, will know exactly how you feel at any given moment. And, happy or sad (and they instinctively know which), will be waiting to give you a great big hug. They are extremely sensitive and rarely get angry. If they do, they forgive and forget faster than any other type of man.

They get into a routine easily and tend to stick to it. They can be a bit of a stick in the mud, and getting them to try something new can be difficult. Appeal to their emotions, and then discuss your predicament. You will feel safer in a new car. You will be more comfortable on a new mattress. Pay attention to his body language. Getting their attention can be as simple as touching them when you are speaking, reiterating that you understand exactly how he feels. Guaranteed that he'll listen to anything you have to say.

One thing a feeling person can't stand is change. Why? Because change is uncomfortable and God forbid they are uncomfortable. If change is in the venue, then you have to do everything in your power to get him to believe that it won't dramatically impact his regular routine. Once he understands that he'll be more apt to go along willingly.

How to Impress a Feeling Man

Remember the old saying about the way to a man's heart is through his stomach? Well, it was written for a feeling man. He can be quite moody, and one of the ways in which he soothes himself is with food. You can just mention making his favorite dish and he'll perk right up.

Anything of importance that you have to say to him should be done in private where you can touch him—even if it's just holding his hand or rubbing his arm. He likes to be touched and held and comforted physically. The nice thing is you don't have to worry about how you look. He'll love you despite your flaws, including when you wake up in the morning with a hangover and your face resembles a punching bag. He is quite capable of pulling your dehydrated self back together with a hug and a kind word. His intuition is extremely strong, so if you're faking your feeling for him, he'll smell it a mile away.

If you really want to knock his socks off, plan an evening at home, cooking him a fabulous meal. Afterwards, give him a massage. Rub him in all the right ways, using essential oils that cater to his olfactory urges. Aromatherapy was made for this man. You'll see drastic changes in his attitude towards you if you learn to touch him the way he likes to be touched (and get your mind out of the gutter here). If you're going to go out, make it an event that involves his senses. An exhibit of sculptures he can touch, a wine tasting, anything that involves a hot tub.

This man is all about sensations. Touching, tasting, smelling. Combine the three and you have a magic love potion.

Feeling Triggers

Do you have a favorite scent? Good, wear it. Wear it all the time. He can even be turned on by the smell of you, without perfume. In that case, don't wear any. If you don't know what he likes, try out certain scents. One woman loved wearing vanilla on her wrists, but her date always leaned away. Later she found out that he associated the scent of vanilla with his mother.

Scent-sational ideas should spill over to your living environment–scented candles, air freshener, fluffy towels washed in rain scented detergent, and soft sheets you dab with rose oil.

Key characteristics:

- Pretty introverted
- They stay to themselves
- Not impulsive; will think things through carefully before making a decision
- Generally, they speak at a slower pace
- Good memories
- Plans events carefully and pays attention to meticulous details

Key careers:

- Medical professional
- Animal trainer
- Therapist
- Teacher
- Bartender

Key words to use:

- How does that feel to you?
- It touched me deeply.
- I sense that you don't feel good.
- I understand how you feel.
- I love touching your hair.

Key environment:

- Comfortable is key (the feeling man loves his recliner)
- Calm and peaceful; loud neighbors that fight all the time will drive him nuts

THE MOST INFLUENTIAL LANGUAGE?

First of all, what exactly is meant by most influential? It's the language in which you can influence a person the most, one in which you can get them to drop their defenses and open up. In order for this to occur most effectively, this entails some sensitivity on both parts. In other words, the person must relate to you and to themselves in a feeling state of mind.

How do you do that, especially if they are predominantly visual, the least like a feeling person? As stated before, all of us have moved across planes of languages (even if you've never been to Spain). Sorry, I digress. What you must do is go there yourself. Not Spain, but to a feeling state of mind, which is not nearly as difficult as one may think.

Simply recall an emotional issue, such as the last time you received bad news—chances are you immediately went to a feeling state. Your eyes dropped down, your speech slowed, and your body moved at a decreased speed. In the movies, you'll see investigators do this to obtain information. They corner a suspect and mention the deceased. This works particularly well if it's a family member. Don't you want to catch the person who killed your brother? Instantly, they are drawn into themselves and their emotions.

By becoming serious yourself, lowering your voice and bringing up a meaningful topic, the other person follows suit. They begin to mirror you, whether they know it or not. That's why the expression, "I don't want to be around her, she's such a downer," holds credence. When you are around someone deeply depressed, you tend to take on the same attributes. Do not get depressed, but do become introspective. You will elicit the same with whom you are conversing. Done in a quiet, private environment this gives the person permission to open up about real issues. Then you can gather the most information about who and what a person is truly made of.

This works if you're dealing with a person one-on-one, but what if you're speaking to a group? The best way to reach an audience is to touch upon all three. For instance, you would say, "If you think this looks like a good idea, you're right. It not only sounds good, but also feels good." Otherwise, stick with the visual, and the majority will see things your way.

WHAT IF YOU SPEAK A DIFFERENT LANGUAGE?

Let's see, you're the auditory type that doesn't like a lot of noise. You seek out peace and quiet. Unfortunately, the man you just met is visual. He doesn't care how loud things get because he's moving a mile a minute trying to show you just how much fun you can have together. Are you doomed before you begin? Of course not. It helps if you both speak the same language, but it's not necessary, only that you be aware of who speaks what. In fact, conversing congruently can be a hindrance. You can be so much alike that you drive each other crazy.

The purpose of learning which plane a person navigates upon is to understand their problems more effectively and increase your level of communication. In this manner, your language will compliment theirs, and you will know when to compromise, or which approach to take when making a point. Or, trying to get them to do exactly what you want them to do. Never out of the question.

CHAPTER THIRTEEN

MIRROR, MIRROR ON THE WALL, SHOW ME HOW TO MAKE ANY MAN LIKE ME BEST OF ALL

One simple rule about people: They like who and what is most like them. Not true, opposites attract, you argue. Yes, they do have a tendency to attract. They just don't have a tendency to stay together. Whether we admit it or not, we seek out people who appeal to us, usually because they appear to be like us. If they act like us, talk like us, walk like us, even look like us, we tend to find them comfortable and relaxing. You are suddenly familiar to them because that source of warmth and safety is associated with you.

Next time you go shopping with your best friend, observe your physical mannerisms. You will probably walk at the same speed, talk at the same speed, stop at the same places, and even tire together. You'll be even more surprised when you realize you finished eating lunch at exactly the same time.

Watch a couple who have been married for years. You'll notice that they walk alike, talk alike, even dress alike. They may not wear the exact same clothing, but the colors will blend, the style will be similar. If you see them in a restaurant, they will move back in their seat simultaneously, order similar types of food, hold their forks in the same manner, and even cut the meat the same way. One will place their elbows on the table, and the other will as well. They talk to each other in similar tones of voice and often finish the other person's sentence. Or when one is speaking, the other will nod in agreement. They are so in tune with each other, they don't even realize that they are unconsciously mirroring each other. Their rapport is so deep, so strong, that they become one in the same person. Once you accomplish this, you become inseparable.

Conversely, if you observe a couple who is not in sync, you can trust that they have problems. Acting dissimilar is a sign of upset, especially is they were previously on the same wavelength. They once did everything together, and now one will say they want to go to Hawaii and the other will say, "Hawaii, I don't want to go to Hawaii. I was thinking more along the lines of New York." They used to play golf, but now when he brings it up she cringes. Mentally they are being drawn farther and farther apart, until the physical can't help but follow.

Mirroring is not as far fetched as it sounds. Salespeople are expert mirrors. They will often go so far as to take on the accent of a potential client. If a salesman tries to sell something to someone who shuts them out by crossing their arms in front of them, he will mimic the person's attitude by closing himself off as well. He may adopt a similar posture and tone of voice. He'll then get the person into a state of agreement, even if it's over something as trivial as the weather.

"Boy, there's a real chill in the air lately, don't you think?" The other guy agrees, "Oh, yeah it's getting cold." Then the salesman may try something like, "You're right, these cars are a bit expensive." He pauses, lowers his arms from his chest, and adds, "How about if I show you something that's just as good, and also more in keeping with your budget?" The potential buyer drops his arms as well and nods, brightening up a bit. By mirroring him, the salesman has reopened the lines of communication.

Attorneys are also adept at mirroring. They will often use the process to build rapport with a witness and the jurors. Politicians use the technique to build their own credibility. They are virtual chameleons when it comes to the crowd and their sociopolitical atmosphere. Parents use it with their children. In trying to get my daughter to take a nap, I would yawn excessively. Counselors and psychologists use it to gain a client's confidence. We often mirror those that we admire and respect. The list is endless, but the point remains the same.

Mirroring is not an exercise in becoming a copycat. You will not only look ridiculous but you will definitely not accomplish your goal. It is a way of concentrating on the other person, enabling you to understand exactly what's going on inside their heads. People who are in different emotional states won't enjoy talking to each other. If they are appearing anxious and nervous, and you are bold and confident, they will feel insecure and intimidated and given the opportunity, they will leave. You have to come down a bit and understand the nervousness to the point where you are appearing to be so as well. You are sympathetic. You understand. Automatically, they will relax. The power you gain is subtle, yet powerful. In other words, one more subliminal step to help you read someone's mind.

What if you get caught? Not a problem! Imitation is the finest form of flattery, right? What man can resist the fact that they can influence poor little you into acting like them? Wow, they have such control over you. They may eat it up, but you will know the truth.

MATCHING MOVEMENTS

Have you been paying attention to body language? I hope so. If not, you will fail mirroring miserably. First, you must become aware of a person's posture, their facial expressions, the tone of their voice, and the rhythm of their breathing. Everything.

If you appear to mirror another on purpose, you will look like a puppet on a string. You must look as if you are unconsciously following their lead. So, let's say a person is tapping their fingers on a table out of boredom. You don't want to appear as if you are a mimic. Instead of tapping your fingers on the table, tap your pen on the arm of your chair, or better yet, tap your foot in the exact same rhythm.

One of the most comforting things we can do is breathe at the same rate as someone else. Remember how safe and secure you felt as a child when your mother held you to her bosom and you could feel and hear her breathing? Nothing made you feel closer. It's probably why after you've made love to a man, you'll find that you will still be breathing "as one." On a less personal basis, keep an eye on someone's shoulders to see the pace at which they are breathing. You don't necessarily have to breathe at exactly the same speed, but if they are mellow and breathing slowly, you will be much more likely to get a response from them.

If you don't want to look obvious, or can't breathe at the same rate, use another action while keeping it at the same speed. If you can stroke them at the same rate, it will have the same effect. Or if you are not in this position, stroke your own arm at the same rate, or a pillow or similar prop. You'll be amazed how comfortable the other person will feel without realizing it.

A person's voice is equally as important. If they are loud and yelling, then yell back. If they are talking softly in almost a whisper, reciprocate. Echoing words and styles of words can be extremely beneficial. We talked about the salesman who adopted his client's accent. Well, they don't stop there, trust me. If the person is using slang, the same slang words will jump out at the other person from his speech as well.

Watch an expert journalist such as Barbara Walters or Larry King on television. They will start to mirror the person they are interviewing. Unconsciously, the interviewee becomes more relaxed and the conversation flows more easily. Suddenly the guest opens up and begins talking as if to a friend.

The one thing you do not want to do is mirror bad behavior. If in the company of someone who curses continually, your mouth will turn just as foul and four letter words will be a noticeable addition to your vernacular. Not necessarily a positive attribute. If you notice yourself doing this, try to not fall into the trap. The other alternative is to turn them around and replace the four letter words with non-offensive words, which still get the idea across. While dining, you can always tell them to fork off.

Don't slouch just because someone else is AS A HABIT. Slouching in order to mirror should last a very short period of time and should not be something you adopt as a natural posture. What if he slouches all the time? Well, he shouldn't. It would be nice if you could break him of that habit. If you can't, and it doesn't bother you, then so be it. We can't change everything we want to about a person, nor should we try. Mirroring is a manner is which to gain a person's confidence, not a manner in which to gain control.

MATCHING MOODS

He's not listening to you? (Big surprise!) Try mirroring his mood. If he's upset, and you come bustling into the room smiling like a ray of sunshine, you will probably not get much of a reaction from him. Most people like to have their feelings validated first, then they can possibly be eased out of the mood they are in. In other words, insisting that they get up and do a dance so that they'll feel better rarely works. Tickling them when they're mad won't work either. Misery loves company, because you trust someone who is agreeing with you. They need to be justified in their feelings, at least initially.

So how do you get someone to snap out of a certain mood? You commiserate. You will get more out of a person by sympathizing and acting out their reactions than you would in any other manner. They warranted a response; therefore, they can drop the mask and explain it. Agree and then try to talk them out of it. If an argument occurs, go back to agreeing and try again.

This not only works with his moods but also with yours. So, he doesn't buy you flowers anymore? Buy him some. If you wish he were more romantic, then you be more romantic. You may mirror people, but don't forget that they mirror you as well. I met a man who wouldn't buy me anything. He just wasn't the type. When he had to, he would, but otherwise forget it. I, on the other hand, love surprising someone with unexpected gifts—things that aren't necessarily expensive, but something I know they needed at the time. This man didn't reciprocate at all. My friends told me I was nuts. What are you doing? But I didn't give up. It took a while, but now I get little presents all the time. Subconsciously, he adopted my spontaneity and generosity.

If you wish he'd learn to cook, then you need to find another man that knows how. Invite the chef over and have him help in the kitchen. Okay, so this may not turn him into Emeril, but he won't feel as threatened, and that's a start. I mean really, a man who cannot stand the heat, will get out of the kitchen anyway. But if he's never been exposed to the stove, why not give it a shot of Sherry?

As with everything, this works both ways. It would be nice if you mirrored his enthusiasm for things he enjoys, even if you don't. If sports are his thing, and you turn into a grumpy old nag every time he turns on a game, you will have problems. First, the man is not for you. Secondly, if he is, then don't antagonize him. Try mirroring his enthusiasm, then leave when the game comes on.

Your attitudes make up your mental being. It's important that you feel the same way he does about morals and values as well. If he likes going to church, then go. Now if this is all sounding like a puppet show, it's not.

If anything, you have the strings. If there weren't a common thread to begin with, you wouldn't be doing the dance in the first place.

CHAPTER FOURTEEN

A DOZEN DON'TS - TWELVE TYPES OF MEN TO AVOID

Hundreds of books have been written on the subject of "types" of men, the majority of which are stereotypical and sexist. Then again, not unlike clichés and old wives' tales, there just may be a nut of truth hidden within the shell. Navigating through life, we cannot help but crash into a few men who possess the same attributes, pigeonholing patterns that enable the phosphorescence of their insides to illuminate a room. A sign is a sign. And no, I am not referring to horoscopes. That may enlighten us to a general description, but unless you know the exact time and place of their birth, then their sun would fall somewhere in the middle of nonsense and their moon in silliness.

Archetypes, not generalizations, create fact, not fiction. I believe Shakespeare claimed there were only a dozen different life stories in existence. The backgrounds may differ, the foregrounds, or the grounds in general, but essentially, they remain constant. By developing your perceptions, it's pretty common to "fit" a man into one or two of the following categories. And why would you want to do that? For one thing, you will be better able to avoid the personality traits incompatible to your own. Understanding someone's issues from the beginning can save you months, possibly years, of heartache and misery. And, if you choose to stick around, you'll be better able to help them if they ask. Basically, you'll know where they are coming from, even if they don't.

The Charmer (aka The Kiss Ass)

The Charmer wants something. And he'll do just about anything to accomplish this goal. Obviously, getting what they want makes them more powerful. So, basically, it's a control issue. What they are trying to do, usually at all costs, is get you to like them, even love them, because it feeds their ego. By manipulating you, they can control you. And if they already know you are smitten, so much the better. How easy it is for the snake to wind its way around your deepest desires. They'll twist and turn things around so much that you can't possibly do anything without checking with them first. But once that occurs, and they've satisfied their insecurity and the need to be loved, they often leave. It really has nothing to do with you; they've been flirting with someone else over your shoulder all along. What they require is more fuel to feed an insatiable desire to be needed, wanted, and loved.

These guys turn the charm on fast and furiously, dishing out compliments sweeter than candy. They frequently employ such devices as double entendres, and sexual innuendoes, in an effort to tell you exactly what you want to hear. It's not beneath them to stretch the truth—or downright lie to you. If caught, they probably won't show much remorse. They have already justified their actions as necessary to their cause, thereby dismissing your anger as an immature hissy fit. If they get caught red handed, they will still try to wiggle their way out of it, determined to make you see why it was necessary for them to take such action in the first place. Listen astutely. You will hear about their needs, and their concerns.

You can often spot The Charmer by the way he moves, usually with his pelvis forward, opening himself up to those around him, thereby appearing confident and secure. He's comfortable with his body and at ease in most situations. Very little will make him nervous. His tone of voice is soft and sexy. When you are talking, he will tilt his head and smile to show interest. If there's a sexual interest, he will half smile, gaze at you longer than usual, then lick his lips. Or they will lower their heads and gaze up at you, making you feel (psychologically), as if you have the upper hand.

Without doubt, Charmers are experts at invading your space. This is so they can accidentally touch you on purpose. Most women crave a man's touch, and this expert seducer will use this tactic to its full advantage. How do you know if he's ever really genuinely interested in you? If he's worth it, stick around without giving too much (if anything) of yourself away. Then see if he sticks around, too.

WHAT TO WATCH FOR: Manipulating others by feigning goodness. Often unfair in business dealings. Excessive flirting.

Peter Pan's Older Brother

Meet Mr. Rebellious all grown up. Man, it's so much easier to act like a boy with an anti-everything, including anti-himself attitude. Why take responsibility when everyone else is acting like an adult? Clinging to his parents, even if they aren't around, makes more sense. Ironic, considering a lot of men who feel this way were abused by their parents, or had parents who were so overbearing their children weren't allowed to eat, sleep, cross the street, or (heaven forbid!) think for themselves. Either way, they were intellectually abandoned. As they got older, they found direction and acceptance from other people. They just never learned to do it for themselves.

Unfortunately, one of the byproducts of the help me, notice me, mentality is someone who will play emotional chicken with you. *If things aren't going to go the way I want them to go, then I'll fall to pieces, and it will be your fault. You are the reason that I am self-destructing.*

Young or old, the rebel wants someone to pay attention to him. Desperately. He is definitely emotionally needy. Judging them is a huge mistake. If you want to be a part of their lives, you must do so unconditionally and without criticism. Give them a lot of attention, notice them, and notice what they are doing. They thrive on the attention. If you love them, they can then love themselves.

WHAT TO WATCH FOR: Extreme insecurity. Neediness. Bitterness.

The Competitor

Whatever you've said, whatever you've done, The Competitor has done it before, and done it better. The trip you took will never surpass the trip they took to the same place. Why, didn't you know, even the weather cooperated. Listen, he'd repaint the Sistine Chapel if well he could. If pushed to acknowledge their need to supercede, The Competitor shifts gears faster than a Ferrari, until they, once again, prevail, even if this requires that you not get a word in edgewise. You may say a rose is a rose by no other name, and he'll respond with, "That's simply not true. The genus for a rose is Rosa."

A big, black jealousy monster lurks in the corner of his soul, hidden behind a blatant desire to exceed anyone else's expectations. He bites big time, with teeth that spill poison into the veins of anyone entering The Competitor's personal life. Without doubt, whatever you choose to do, right down to dressing for the occasion, you didn't do it as well as he could. This can get pretty damned annoying. The criticism, especially of something you said and forgot about (they remember things that can later be used as ammunition), can cause quite a puddle of confusion you can't quite figure out how to mop up. Do not try. The rigid posture is mirrored by their mentality. They do not bend. In the beginning, they won't even stand too close, maintaining a proper distance to circumspect the situation, eyes darting around, taking in everything around them.

Be content to play second fiddle, or forget it.

WHAT TO WATCH FOR: Undermining you, or anyone else for that matter. Hard to please. This is the quintessential got to keep up with the Jones type, and until they do, they are rarely satisfied.

The Suffering Servant

Everything I do, I do because I love you. Sound familiar? The problem is, it's not so much that The Suffering Servant is doing whatever it is they are doing because they love you. Quite the contrary. Selfish streaks run down the paint camouflaging the facade. This is the type who, before an utterance of any form of a commitment, gallops, pants, rushes over to your house after work everyday to walk your dog and cook you dinner. Surely you are too busy, with no time to yourself, and completely unable to get everything done when you are trying to get ahead. Not to mention the fact that you'll be indebted to them.

For the most part, they are literally dying to take care of you, sacrificing their own time, money, mental activity, and blood to accommodate you. Fine with them as, generally speaking, they're not looking to amount to much on their own. They'd much rather make themselves indispensable to someone else who is going to succeed for them. Proceed with caution, as the other side of the coin reveals a sick, whining soul, tired of being used and abused. Then flip it again and get a real head's up. The fact that they want you, need you, to love them stems from a lack of love during their childhood. Still emotionally starved for affection, they crave attention. "Love me, love me, please love me," they finally scream aloud.

Now that they jumped overboard, they expect you to toss them a life raft equipped with a mini bar. Their voice remains calm and agreeable, for they aim to please, remember? Although, tantamount to masochism, they seek not an argument, only more attention. Quite often, they hunch their shoulders while waiting for a victim to arrive, the posture aiding in their ability to withdraw from the world. If they maintain a suitable hiding place, no one can walk all over them. Alas, the master abandons the slave for a more suitable suitor.

Gently show them that they don't necessarily have to bend over backwards at their own expense, that they're worth more than that. Being helpful and of service to the community and the people in it is a kind and compassionate thing, different from being a doormat.

There's also one more thing I have to add here. It might sound strange at first, but a large majority of women don't like men who are too nice. Hear me out. I certainly had my share of horrible experiences with men, including family, old boyfriends, game players, tyrants, and you name it. I, more than anyone I can think of, want a man to treat me with consideration and respect. But the trouble is, if a guy you just met is too nice, you not only get suspicious and wonder why but also subconsciously back away when the challenge ended before it began. Somewhere in between his rushing around to pick up your laundry and your groceries, you lost interest.

My guess is that it has something to do with the many movies we've watched since we were oh, I don't know, ten, in which the handsome hero is never really that nice until he meets the girl (and she makes him that way). Otherwise, he's just a guy who can't get a girl. Whatever the reasons, don't drop a man because he's considerate so that you can obsess over one determined to treat you like dirt and never returns your calls.

WHAT TO WATCH FOR: Getting upset about things they can't fix, but then refusing to get out there and do something about it. Constantly complaining about being overworked and underpaid. Gets too personal too quickly.

The Tyrant

Picture a GQ type on a big, fat power trip. Not unlike his lesser counterpart, the Butch Bully (not even worth bringing in up in this book, or in your life), The Tyrant remains fundamentally scared. You can bet a lot of anger is packed into the baggage they carry around with them. (If you get close enough, you can smell what's inside, too.)

You can tell they're coming by the heaviness of their gait. Whether they are mad at the moment or not (and, guess what, they are), they furrow their brows and scowl at you with tight lips and hands clenched into fists. Their voice bellows aggressively, while their expression remains hard and callous. Unless you are extremely domineering, now would be the time to disappear. Otherwise, you become an asset, lending credibility to their actions.

Before you hand over the steering wheel in this relationship, consider the fact that you won't be able to drive again. It goes without saying that they know how to run your life better than you do. Don't worry, they remind you of this constantly, whether you want them to or not. The longer you go along with them, the harder it will be to break free. They then have you exactly where they want you to be and will continue to exercise their ability to masterfully manipulate your emotions by being even more arrogant.

It goes without saying that you can't help these people. For one thing, why would you want to? The only way to match up to them is through sheer force. You have to stand up to them in order to gain their respect. You literally have to hit them over the head with a two-by-four to get them to see that hurting people is not how you get them to love you. Even then, they may simply feign understanding and continue doing exactly what they've been doing. The truth hurts, but it is not their truth, so they continue to fight back.

The irony is that they want to be loved. But how can you love them if you can't get close to them? Then the very fact that no one does justifies their behavior. They become even more verbally and physically abusive.

There's a whole lot of self-inflicted pain going on here. Somehow, the world has passed them up. The break they should have gotten simply never appeared. So, what better way to avoid facing their own demons than by creating some for somebody else? Run. And whatever you do, don't look back.

WHAT TO WATCH FOR: Using power trips to control you. Dishonesty and corruption in their business dealings. Using anger as a weapon, and as a shield. Emotional and physical abuse.

The Victim

First of all, let's get one thing clear: a person does not have to be victimized to be a victim. The truth is most haven't been. Or they haven't been victimized any more than the normal amount. That is to say, we've all been guilty of being The Victim at some time or another in our life. A devastating event or emotionally crippling trauma transpires and we need someone to lean on. But that's entirely different from someone who lives for it. Get out the violins, because here he comes. It's time for the tragic song and dance, undoubtedly hitting epic proportions. What would drama be without actors giving commercials about it, or a victim thriving on it?

This is the poor me attitude exemplified. Don't feel so bad for them, and whatever you do, don't try to rescue them. Bottom line here: they count on exactly that. If they keep complaining, maybe someone else will fix whatever problem it is they have. Sounds a lot like laziness, doesn't it?

You can tell The Victim by the way they move about. They are often hunched over from lack of self-confidence, which causes them to bump into things, drop things and hurt themselves. They visit emergency rooms with alarming frequency.

If so inclined, go ahead and offer The Victim a possible solution to the problem he is having. What you will hear is a "yeah, but . . . " reply. They are famous for the yeah, buts. They already tried whatever solution you presented, or there's more to it than you could possibly fathom. As you will see, they not only like the problem, they have fallen in love with the problem. They live for the drama. Without a crisis what would they do? How else will they get attention? After all, this is cause for everyone to stop and take notice of their story. A story, by the way, which is told from one perspective. Their own. It's a myth they grew so attached to they can't help but recite it endlessly to everyone they meet. The God's conspired against this mere mortal. How sad.

Victims will suck you dry. Not necessarily monetarily but emotionally. Quite often, the cause of their pain is based upon a loss of some kind—a job, a person, it doesn't matter. It could be the big break they thought they should get and didn't. Point is they focus on the negative. They haven't figured out the payoff in changing. In a sense, they like being stuck.

Keep your distance. Don't even stand too close, or they'll exhaust you. Offer solutions if you must, but don't buy into their sob story. Once you commiserate, you are doomed. Doomed, I tell you. Before long, they'll be sleeping on your couch and emptying your refrigerator.

WHAT TO WATCH FOR: Using the poor me attitude to gain sympathy from others. Always acting helpless.

The Perfectionist

Ever meet a lizard? They jump up, run really fast. Freeze. Observe any creature of the wild, including The Perfectionist, and you will note the similarities. They can be as quick as a blink, vanishing faster than steam on a hot sidewalk, or become statues of stone.

The Perfectionist self-sabotages himself, constantly setting himself up for disappointment, much like the skydiver who never makes the jump because the parachute has a fold out of place, or a diver who never leaves the cliff because the water is never the right temperature. Perfectionism paralysis sets in.

Point it out and see what happens. They blow it off by blaming someone else. Somebody else trapped them in this less than perfect life because no matter how good it is, it can always be better—one of the most potent lies The Perfectionist tells himself. There must be a better job out there, a better woman, a better apartment, or a better whatever. So, he won't hang the pictures in his office, or redecorate the apartment, or even get serious with a woman for fear there may be a more suitable one right around the next corner.

What's this? It's called stalling. Perfectionists prefer procrastinating. It's easier to stay safe and stuck than it is to go out there and take a chance.

They have yet to hear the expression, "Winners don't wait for chances; they take them." The outcome is anger and frustration.

Convincing The Perfectionist that change is a good thing may not be that difficult to accomplish, as long as he hasn't become what some perfectionists become: narcissistic. Ah yes, if he's so interested in being perfect this is often the case. Suddenly, the world revolves around them and so do their conversations. If per chance you veer onto another subject, for instance, say yourself, my dear, they will become bored and uninterested. They believe they are important because they are perfect. This also makes them sought after and popular. Right? Hence an unwarranted sense of entitlement clouds the mind like a fog in a dream.

If you hang around, then at least you know what to buy them for Christmas. A mirror will always do. Just remember, there's only room for one image.

WHAT TO WATCH FOR: Can get overly uptight over the silliest, most trivial, matters. Favorite saying: "If you're going to do it, do it right." Taking over projects, because, after all, only they can do it properly.

The Egghead

Sometimes a man can be too smart for his own good. Hear me out. The last gentleman referenced had perfectionist paralysis, which, if not treated develops into analysis paralysis. Eggheads are so smart that they can't stop thinking. They figure the problem out, then go over it again and again and again, and when they reach a conclusion they'll start over to make sure they reached the right one. In so doing, they become moody and sardonic.

These guys talk too much, tongues wagging like a rodeo champion about things like rudimentary Japanese, basic astronomy, intermediate history, and advanced geography, not to mention quantum physics, the literary arts, and of course (how could we forget!), philosophy.

There's that type and the other, more common one, that doesn't say anything at all, no matter how hard you try to get them out of their shell. (You could throw an egg at it.) That's because they're having all of these long conversations with themselves in their head. The problem here is that they can get pretty boiled up by all of this over thinking, which will force them to put off making any decisions until they are thoroughly convinced that they are doing the right thing. The other problem is that their head gets so big that they can't find their heart. Logical, everything must be logical, and reasonable, leaving very little room for emotions. Suddenly they lose touch with reality. They forget about the simple things in life, like laughing. It may be difficult to convince them that there is more to socializing than a Mensa meeting.

Another repercussion of a particularly high I.Q. is the need to overachieve. But bear in mind that the outcome is not necessarily the goal. It's the praise that comes with it. An award without a ceremony wouldn't cut it.

Remember, thinking can be hazardous to your health. If you are not careful, it can cause all kinds of ailments, masquerading as neurotic behavior. Detonations of antagonism and lambasting criticism explode around them like minefields. Those who are of an inferior mindset shall be killed off. Show no mercy to these inarticulate, naïve, and tedious types. Blow them to smithereens!

To comprehend the Egghead may mean that you end up with some on yours. Egg, on the head. Or the face. A brave soul may venture forth into this land of intellectual idealism, but only if you can take their hand once in a while and show them another land of the living. Otherwise, they begin to worship their brain, which is almost as bad as not having one.

WHAT TO WATCH FOR: They have a tendency to get upset with people who are not as savvy as they are. Often feel threatened or insecure for no reason at all.

The Religious Fanatic

Holy cannoli, these guys can sound as smooth as a Baptist preacher's rant. Whether a religious fanatic belongs to a certain religion or not is beside the point. Sometimes they don't belong to any. The point is, however, that they believe, without doubt, that they are righteous. They are God's gift to the world, sent here for the sole purpose of transforming your sorry self.

The game plan: convert your way of thinking into theirs. How you manage your time, the way you dress, how you pay your bills, cook, clean, think, will be subject to scrutiny. If The Religious Fanatic happens to refrain from indulging in red meat, then by God, you should, too. They'll harp on the subject of meatless meals, nag you about cholesterol and calories, send you articles from obscure magazines, or force you to dine exclusively at vegetarian restaurants, until you give in. Not exactly a subtle sell.

They can be more judgmental than the average person because if you're not exactly like them, viewing the world through their pious eyes, you must be crazy. They can be downright nasty if, for instance, you continue to drink (which they may drive you to), and they don't. There is no leeway for this kind of behavior, even if it means resorting to the soapbox. Here comes the bellicose puffery. By getting you to go along with how they view the world, it makes that world that much more real, and consequently that much more important.

Believing in something too much is just as bad as believing in nothing at all. Fortunately, a truly spiritual man will not impose his beliefs on you, trying to recruit you into his way of worship—or into his way of anything. There's the man you want. The Religious Fanatic is more compatible with someone who shares their beliefs to begin with.

WHAT TO WATCH FOR: Putting others down, especially if they do not believe as they believe. Over-generalizing about groups of people. Prejudicial points of view.

The King

Guessing this guy is a snob? Well, you would definitely be right. If you can get their nose down from up in the air long enough, you'd see it in their eyes. Whether The King has money, used to have money, or pretends to have money is irrelevant. The operative word remains money and obsessing over it. See, somehow or another they must defend who and what they are, which is rich (even if they aren't). Why? Because wealth and respect are synonymous to The King, much like love and whining are to The Princess. The importance of The King reigns supreme. So much so, they go to great lengths to create the illusion, with a certain air that surrounds them—an air that generally stinks of judgment, unreasonableness, sarcasm, elitism, and possibly racism.

Accordingly, maintaining an elevated stature requires putting people in their place. They use various techniques to accomplish this, but I can tell you right now that none are difficult to spot. Only the deaf could not hear the condescending tone they assume whilst pontificating for hours on subjects too sophisticated for the common ear, thence cutting you off if you voice an opinion. Only the blind could not see the stiff posture they assume, and the rigid manner in which they hold themselves. They raise their chin, and smile sarcastically, eyelids half closed, eyebrows raised when listening to someone else speak. Clearly making it apparent that you have no idea what you are talking about.

Now, some good news. The King requires no assistance from his minions. Mostly because Kings don't think they need help, and even if they did, admitting it would be like committing emotional hari-kari. Lord forbid, they stoop as low as middle class. On the other side of the velvet curtain, however, they don't wish to be left alone. The King needs his people. Solitude is not a word in their ostentatious vocabulary. Denial is.

After preening extensively in front of the mirror (a favorite past time), The King leisurely searches about for his next audience. Once found, they assume a superior role by standing at a distance and gesticulating grandly while explaining, once again, their superior stance on the subject at hand. These guys also love to make sexually suggestive remarks or movements. After all, they're entitled to whomever they want, right?

Quite often, the royal pains feel compelled to prove how successful they are, how above it all they are. In this case, the penny-pinching caterpillar transforms into an extremely generous butterfly. Watch them fly. Let the bling bling begin. Expect them to lavish you with expensive trips and gifts. No one can blame you for playing in the court now. At least until they get knocked down a notch or two, which if you aren't real royalty or at least Bill Gates, will happen. Not a problem, as you'll be there to tell them just how special they are, with or without all the materialistic madness. Meanwhile, all you really need to do is play along, and feed the illusion that they are God's gift to the world. They may be. After all, aren't we all?

WHAT TO WATCH FOR: Being miserly or overly grandiose. Remember the old saying: A would-be king holds himself above the masses. A true prince walks among them.

The Passive Aggressor

Passive aggressive. Sounds like a bit of an oxymoron, doesn't it? That's because it happens to be one. These people can be annoying (aggressive) by refusing to do things (passive). This type appears happy to agree to do something, but then is slow to get the task done, or worse constantly complains while doing it. No, I'm not talking about liars. They are a different breed. The Passive Aggressor uses a more subtle, less deceiving tactic: mental musculature. Sometimes, it is to control or to punish the other person. These people are obstinate, inefficient, gloomy, moody, and sulky, all while appearing to be cooperative. They tend to be argumentative, especially with those in authority. That's because they are trying to gain control of a situation that is clearly out of their control. Either they are in a position of weakness to begin with, or simply lack the intelligence to make the point.

Quite often, The Passive Aggressor makes a pernicious statement, then covers it up with an, "Oh, but I was just kidding," or "Can't you tell I was just joking?" Okay, let's get one thing clear right now. They are not kidding, and they are not joking.

You can almost see the anger seething inside of them when their jaws tighten and they refuse to open their mouth when they speak. If not, they tend to fidget or bounce their feet and legs up and down at a tremendously high speed. They are nervous, anxious, and accordingly, they can't keep still. Even when they lean forward to show interest in you, they won't be able to hold the position for long.

Passive Aggressors must be in control, without you realizing that they are in control. They command authority by not allowing anyone to get too close, too comfortable. It's difficult for them to give a straight answer to a personal question. If you ask their opinion, they usually won't commit one way or another (until they first find out how the other party feels). Be forewarned. Getting them to open up and allow you into their aggravated minds could kill you.

The best way to handle a Passive Aggressor is to simply give them what they want—attention, affection, letting them "have things their way." Basically, the message they want to hear is that it is okay for them not to meet their obligations and responsibilities, whatever the case may be. Crude as it sounds, that's exactly how they see it. Confronting them about their behavior is more effective, of course, but not generally well received. Trying to identify the real issue and dealing with it is another way of coping.

WHAT TO WATCH FOR: Gossips. Backstabbers. Constantly trying to gain control. Clinging like a leech in heat.

The Wimp

At first The Wimp seems so quiet, so shy. You just want to run up to them and give them a great big hug. Well, before you do, think about what you are getting yourself into. Most Wimps are not only insecure but scared. If they are not using their weakness to their advantage (oh, please come and save me, in the hopes that someone, namely you, will stand up for them), then they use it against themselves.

The most typical version of this type of man is The Wallflower Wimp. The Wallflower Wimp can actually be quite out there. They are seeking approval, and one way to do that is to call attention to, who else? Themselves. They want you to like them. Consequently, they can be quite fun and entertaining. Trouble is they often overcompensate, and their efforts come off as childish and immature. Typically they will stand too close, talk too loud, laugh too hard, and touch inappropriately (although not necessarily sexually). In short, they try too hard to please.

Another version of The Wimp is The Ostrich. This rare bird sticks his head in a hole in the ground. Okay, so maybe it's not a hole, but it may as well be. You can call it the Internet, the television, the sports bar, whatever. The hole. It's where they go so they don't have to face the world. As a result of spending so much time in solitude, some become quite smart. Smart and resentful. They can't help wondering why life passed them by, but the second someone suggests that they do something about it, they stick their head back into the hole.

The Ostrich could use a helping hand. Hopefully one that will take hold of his and show him that it doesn't take all that much courage to get out there and live a little. Really, aren't we all a bit frightened?

A lot of strong, domineering women like wimps. They can control and manipulate them. If that's not what you're looking for, then the best way to get a Wimp to not be a Wimp is to encourage him. They need their confidence built up. And with a little tenderness and loving care, that shouldn't be too difficult to do. Plus, the more often they get out there, the easier it will be.

WHAT TO WATCH FOR: Leaning on you for emotional or financial support. Or worse, both.

CHAPTER FIFTEEN

HOW TO SPOT A SOCIOPATH

"Our society distrusts the term 'evil.' It has an almost biblical ring to it—something we believe in (or not), but never actually understand. We prefer scientific-sounding terms, such as sociopath." —Andrew Vachss.

Volumes can, and have, been written on the subject of psychotics by far more qualified people than I. Still, there remains no definitive definition. Analyzing the personality of a sociopath or psychopath can take a lifetime because no two are alike.

Are there signs? Clues? I mean, you really can't walk up and ask if they are one. You have to get to know enough about them pretty quickly to determine if there is the slightest hint that a man might be dangerous. Fear is our inborn alarm system when it comes to such situations, and it should never be ignored.

If you go back and take a good hard look at some of the serial killers of the past, you'll see that on the surface they appeared to be nice, ordinary gentlemen. Except these seemingly unobtrusive men took to violence like duct to tape. Studies have proven that most sociopaths are men, and, regrettably, they are everywhere. They are in line behind you at the grocery store, at the bookstore looking at books, in the pharmacy waiting for a prescription, and picking up milk at the grocery store. Unfortunately, not enough of them are in prison. Only forty percent of prison inmates were

181

diagnosed as sociopaths, with a whopping ninety percent of those who committed violent crimes.

One of the problems of detecting psychotics is that they come from all walks of life. It is said that roughly twenty percent are found in positions such as law enforcement. As Jungian author Guggenbuhl-Craig said, " . . . those who cannot love want power." Thus, not only will they take the shape of a drug addict but also a well-educated person holding a high position in our communities and society in general. That's fine, as the majority will not run amuck slitting women's throats for fun. And, if they did, chances are they would not choose such circumspect circumstances. But if you meet one at a party, and invite him over for a nightcap, you'd better know exactly what you are up against.

The most common trait amongst sociopaths is narcissism. Sociopaths only care about themselves. Period, the end. They want what they want, and they mean to get it at anyone else's expense. This is easy for them to do, as they don't have a conscious. They packed it up and shipped it off with a used flying carpet salesman. They can justify their actions no matter how senseless they seem.

If you spot that kind of power burning in someone's eyes (which is where it will appear most prominently), then watch out. Researchers discovered that the psychopath often glances at a person with reptilian type eyes, much like a predator before it consumes its prey. Unfortunately, most women confuse this for a sign of sexuality and are actually flattered by the attention.

Guilt is a word (and emotion) sociopaths cannot comprehend. Even if they admit to making a mistake, someone or something else was to blame. At least, they'll find a way to attribute it as such, even if it goes back to dear old mom.

Obviously, if there is any kind of physical abuse or mental abuse lurking in their background, take heed. Children who were abused often grow up to be adults that abuse others. This doesn't necessarily have to be directed to you either. If they tell you they would love to poison the dog next door, they probably could, or worse would. Don't take any chances. Besides, if they are that interested in themselves, they won't pay attention to you anyway. They'd rather spend time talking about themselves, to themselves, with themselves. Who needs it?

All of this sounds pretty negative, right? That's because it is. It's not easy to spot someone with potential problems. They camouflage their true feelings, intentions, and motives, frequently underneath a blanket of money—a personality trait transparent among winners. One thing to remember is that damaged people attract damaged people. So, take care of your own issues and start magnetizing mature, grownup men who are not looking for someone to come along and complete them but rather someone to come along and compliment them.

Key Signs for Spotting the Antisocial Personality:

- Superficially charming (can really turn it on when necessary), immediately inspiring trust and confidence
- Excellent insight into the needs and weaknesses of others
- Boyishly rebellious
- Lack of empathy, compassion, guilt, or remorse
- Absence of anxiety (doesn't learn from his mistakes and doesn't care)
- Approaches problems in a manipulative manner, justifying their actions by stating that their victim would do the same
- Generally unreliable
- Lack of insight into the consequences of their actions
- Are under the impression that they are powerful people
- Brags about criminal behavior or legal problems for which they were never caught
- Hates to lose
- Refuses to comply with rules (dress codes, no smoking, etc.)
- Will quit a job, or walk away from a situation, impulsively
- Brags about his sexuality
- Seeks thrills, and has a tendency not to look before they leap
- Makes promises they never keep

PART THREE

THE POWER OF POSSIBILITIES

"Learning is acquired by reading books, but the much more necessary learning, the knowledge of the world, is only to be acquired by reading men, and studying all the various editions of them." –Lord Chesterfield, "Letters to His Son"

CHAPTER SIXTEEN

EXPANDING YOUR INTUITION: STEPPING INSIDE A MAN'S MIND

A revolution is taking place on this planet—a revolution of the mind. It is a time when we seek to delve deeper into the mysteries of the secrets hidden within the subconscious mind and enter into a new paradigm. No longer is it considered inappropriate to limit logic and uphold a so-called "scientific method" as our only means of guiding our lives. The fact that life is a mystery is no longer such a mystery after all.

The general public, the essential core, is now open to relying upon a perception and understanding that is not necessarily visible to the naked eye. Linear thinking no longer dictates the totality of our definitive, objective reality. Intuition, faith, and prayer are no longer banished to the realm of the mystical, or ignored completely by religious dogma, but rather considered reliable methods for healing and decision making. The possibility of endless possibilities exists, and the window that looks out to the edge of infinity has opened up into our world.

When this transpired, physicists discovered what spiritual teachers knew all along—that our physical existence consists of nothing more than a force called energy. Solid matter isn't solid at all; it is comprised of smaller particles inside of other particles. If we look through a powerful microscope at anything solid, we would see an infinite number of tiny vibrating particles, which if brought down to its truest essence, is made up of more particles, more commonly known as energy.

How many times have you heard a detective declare that in order to catch a criminal, they must first think like one? He steps inside the criminal's mind by becoming so attuned to him that the officer actually becomes the offender. Some version of the criminal's thoughts transfer to the detective, just as quantum energy does. It literally leaps between two points without stopping anywhere in between. Scientists proved that. Perhaps they will get a jump on our thoughts next.

These shadowy phantoms of our ideas are not as bizarre, or as scary, as one might imagine. Native American Indians used this concept to communicate with animals. To understand the wisdom of an eagle, they would open themselves up and allow the eagle's vibrations to become one with their own. They respected the revelations they received as part of the flow of imagery from a higher source, not fantasy. As the American Indian meditated, the eagle's thoughts and feelings were assumed by him, the effect of these messages freely flowing through his imagination. They would use the same method to communicate with inanimate objects as well—a rock, a piece of driftwood, a seashell, a lock of hair.

Sound a bit implausible? Consider this. If our brain activity is constantly changing, altering chemicals made of molecules and atoms, perhaps we are not that different from that rock, or piece of driftwood, or seashell. Thinking is a quantum activity, which is why it allows us to control the laws of nature. This is not the magic carpet ride of thinking but rather the form of thought that allows a man to walk on fire. He thinks he can walk on fire, and so he can. Therefore, does this not imply that the fire understands him, as much as he understands the fire? It sounds like a radical paradigm, but in reality, it is one we visit frequently. It's the stamp of influence you place upon your own thinking. Put in those terms, it doesn't sound like there's anything supernatural about it. That's because there isn't. We all sense the rhythm of our environment in a way that's more profound than we realize. How else can we drink from a golden fountain of sunshine?

It is not necessary to transform yourself into a metaphysical master, or even spiritualist, in order to delve inside a man's mind. All you really have to do is believe that the possibility exists. Allow his energy to enter into your own, and you'll be surprised by what you discover. This is not exercising any kind of mind control. It is an understanding that the world is really inside of us, not outside of us. By engaging in a creative act with every exchange of energy, we bridge the gulf all the time. Can we not both sit on the river bed and get in the water simultaneously? In the thick of things, we cannot imagine this. But if we step back, we view our deeper intelligence. We create with God (or the Higher Power of your choice). Our thoughts dance and move incisively together, aware of where they will step next into the rich matrix of possible outcomes.

As Carl Jung believed, in a deep inner subconscious level we are all linked. You can be as close to somebody standing next to you as somebody ten thousand miles away. This means that whether we like it or not, our thoughts affect other people, just as much as our actions. Perhaps more so, for our thoughts move quickly and manifest instantly. Actions are nothing more than the external manifestation of those ideas and subconscious impulses. Any act we undertake started with a reason, with a desire. If you go to the bathroom, it started with your bladder banging on a nerve. If you eat, chances are your stomach rumbled first. It doesn't matter what you do, you thought about it first. By keeping this in mind, you will move more deeply into the unmanifest domain. Blurry edges and uncertain outcomes become nonexistent.

Now a word about energy. The law goes like this: Energy will attract energy of a similar quality and vibration. It's a virtual magnet. So basically, "As you sow, so shall you reap," is literal. Take it personally, because what you think about the most and what you believe the most are exactly what you draw into your life.

That said, here's an even more intimidating idea. If thoughts are energy, then you don't have to consciously act it out to make it manifest. Just having the thought is enough. If you think you are overweight, you will be, even if you consciously continue to diet. If you think you are beautiful, you will be. Our real feelings, secret feelings, originate in the mind and are resonating messages beneath the surface continuously. Our own awareness is what creates the boundaries of our past, present, and future. They are formed in consciousness and destroyed in consciousness. Even our most basic decisions are open to choice. This exact moment is where this occurs and you transcend the past and future (mere illusions, which are distracting at best), as it is a new beginning, fresh, and as devoid of judgment as a newborn child.

One day, words like psychic, clairvoyant, and mystic will no longer exist. Once the door to wisdom opens, we can dive beneath the surface of life into the infinity of our own minds. Once we understand that God's mind is multi-dimensional, then so is ours. Nothing is lost. Have you ever walked into a room after two people have had an argument and felt disturbed, anxious? You want to leave. (By the way, if they keep it up pretty soon the plants die, the animals get sick, the people get sick, yet no one attributes it to the black cloud of emotional pollution suffocating the air.)

Our energy is where everything is explained—charisma, power, everything. When two people meet, you can almost see the sparks fly. Shards of impressions and imprints shoot outward and mingle together, speaking in the language of light. Haven't you ever had the experience of others reacting to you for no apparent reason? What they're picking up on is the energy you emit. Even if they can't see it, or put it into words, they feel it, and subliminally, they form an opinion. People can disguise their looks, their words, their actions. But they can't conceal their energy.

It's time to claim that power. It's already in each and every one of us. All you have to do is tap into it. Keep your mind open and clear. Demand that each and every one of your faculties engage in a total and complete understanding of what you are feeling. Part of reading into someone is simply insisting that you can. It's your right. Now it's time to exercise that right.

SILENT LISTENING

Internal conversations take place inside a person's mind all day long. Possibly all night long. Whether we recognize it or not, we talk to ourselves. We tell ourselves things. And we hear things. I am not referring to mental illness, as this is serious and requires medical treatment. What I am discussing is a "normal" person's ability to conceive new ideas. Thoughts form as a result of stored information inside the neurons in our brains. If this is the case, then how does anyone come up with anything new? Are we not simply combining and recombining the tried and true? New thoughts do not originate in the brain. They originate in the mind, a powerful place, full of breakthroughs, insights, and inspiration.

The mind constantly evolves. Some hidden intelligence (I refer to as God, but please don't be offended) seems to know when and where to transform us, usually when we least expect it. This amazing bio-computer tells us how, turning over data faster than Donald Trump turns over money. So, who are we listening to? Ourselves? For the most part, yes, as co-creator, we are. But sometimes our intuitive self speaks in fragmented words or disjointed images. And, sometimes they make absolutely no sense. Guess what? It doesn't matter. It's still true. If something inside of you warns not to get on an airplane, or make that phone call, or get into that car, then don't.

If you are ever at a point where you are not certain what to do, where to go, why or how, particularly if the situation gives you a fearful feeling, what should you do? Ask. You don't have to ask audibly, just internally. Be specific. *Will I be happy with the man I just met?* You could get a lobotomy, and you would definitely be happy with him.

Will we ever be without money? He could lose his job and get unemployment, so you wouldn't really be without money, now would you?

Should I marry this man? That's a really bad question to ask. Should is relative. That's because the question should be based on criteria, stipulated by your unique set of circumstances. Is security the main concern? Companionship? *If I marry him, will I be able to stay home and raise children?* There are too many variables. The better question would be to ask what kind of life you would create together and see what comes to you. How do your feel? What do you hear, smell? What are you remembering?

If you're not sure what you'd like to know, simply find out if this is the kind of person you'd like to have in your life (as a friend, a lover, or just an acquaintance). What are the qualities you admire most in this person? What could you learn from this person? What does this person need to do to be more fulfilled in his life? What would challenge this person?

The simplest questions you can ask your inner self involve a yes/no situation. *Will I like working with this man? Is he planning to ask me out again?* Just remember that yes and no are simplistic answers to simplistic questions. That means that they can be subjective and can change with the slightest element, like the weather. But for the time being, the answer you receive is true and correct.

All the information is there for the asking. It already exists. In a sense, reading people in this manner is a two-step process, not unlike dreaming, waking up, and then rigorously interpreting the answers in perspective to the information you desired. Our subconscious mind speaks to us in symbols and images. If you have never read Carl Jung's book, *Man and His Symbols,* you should. In it, you will be reminded of our subconscious archetypes and the complexity of their nature in terms of our psychological makeup.

The book is not only interesting but also the pictures are cool. Okay, I'm just kidding. What I mean is that you don't have to have a doctorate in psychology to understand it. So, don't let it frighten you. Analyzing dreams is essential to helping you decipher your visions. Although they have less depth than fog, they reach us on our deepest level. Think of them as angels without the wings.

Learn to scrutinize the symbols as they relate to you directly. For instance, you may be heading for a waterfall in your dream, and you decide that signifies danger ahead. If you are driving to the waterfall, it could be that you are headed in that direction faster than you realized. Who is in the car with you? Are they driving and therefore responsible? What was the weather like? Pay attention to every minor detail. If you're not sure what it means, again ask. *I am going to the waterfall, because . . .* and let your subconscious mind fill in the blank. Each component is a portion of the sentence your subconscious is trying to convey to you, so don't leave any rock unturned. In fact, what does the rock mean?

Let's say you'd like to know if a man might propose marriage to you (remember be specific). You close your eyes and see a rollercoaster crashing downward, you're screaming with that rush of fear and pleasure, your throat constricts, and your eyeballs swim in delirium. Yes, yes, but it will be an exhilarating ride. Where was your attention placed in time? In the present? The distant future? At what point did the rollercoaster settle down, and how did you feel? Warm and flushed, or cold and chilled?

If you ask for a sign of some sort while perfectly wide awake, your subconscious will accommodate you. Say you really want to know if you should venture into this business deal with a particular person. You ask for a sign. You look around and see a spider spinning a web. It doesn't even have to be a real spider. Perhaps you closed your eyes and that's what came to mind. Now, put yourself right in the picture. Is it happening now? Later? Are you hot, cold? Is the spider black or white? Is the picture in color? Is the web complex? Is the spider deadly? Would you conduct business with this spider?

Perhaps a symbol comes to you and you don't know what it means. That's okay, too. Do not force the issue because then you are simply making answers up, and that defeats the purpose. You ask for instructions and see a billboard. You know it should mean something, but what? Trust, and have faith. The answer will come to you. If not, move on and ask again later.

It would be nice if the solution to our inner questions came to us in a voice that sounded like God. Do not discount this, for God will speak to you if you ask Him to. But if that's not the case, He may send a response in a different manner. The blessing could be a book, a movie, or scene from one on television, a card, a song. The possibilities are endless. Or, you may just close your eyes and the answer will flash before you, as if in a dream. Remember, dreams are drawn upon past experience. It's like putting old wine in new bottles.

Aristotle once said that in order to become a good interpreter of dreams, one must learn to recognize "resemblances." I believe that what he meant was that our images occur to us in patterns. In other words, what we are feeling, hearing, seeing, or smelling, in that dream state, will naturally form its own theme. Let's say you dream about the fairy tale, *The Princess and the Pea*. The next morning you wake up and your neck is sore and aching. Well, you should interpret this as being uncomfortable pretending to be something you are not. You will have to determine which situation in your life is making you feel that way and act accordingly. Otherwise, it will continue to be a pain in the neck. Literally.

Symbols mean different things to different people. Some might believe a black cat signifies danger, mysticism, or even witchcraft. I, however, had a black cat named Midnight who was an absolute nut and a joy to behold. She always made me feel better. So, if I see a black cat, I would interpret it as comfort and security, not danger. Context must also be taken into consideration. Rain may signify pleasure if I see myself wrapped up in a blanket on a couch with a date, or danger if I'm driving in a car and the road is slick, and the car veers like a snake.

This is why I believe dream dictionaries are pointless. They cannot possibly be accurate, are not accurate, as they determine the substantive significance of an image by rote. Albeit there are certain archetypal metaphors that hold a common denominator in terms of interpretation, but for the most part, our own thoughts and impressions are personal and hold special meaning to us alone.

You don't need a straight answer. In fact, what you're doing is so nonlinear that odds are you won't get one. What you will get is a sense and impression. All of your thoughts, your feelings, your memories that come shooting into your mind, will be providing you with information. Important information. Do not dismiss anything, no matter how irrelevant it seems.

Allow one vision to lead to another, allowing an uninterrupted flow. You can assemble, interpret, and verify later. For example, if you are at dinner with a man, or in a car, or somewhere where you can take a minute to clear your mind and hold him there, you can then ask the question for which you'd like an answer. Say, for instance, you'd like to find out if you'll end up having a serious relationship with this man. Then you see rain, which turns into a bathtub full of water and your mother screaming at you. This brings to mind the time you almost drowned in the bathtub when you were four years old and how upset your mother was. Well, this is a pretty portentous indication. At this time, it's not looking so good. He obviously suffocates you or smothers you in some other way. Do not get upset. God knows what He's doing.

If a question does not come to mind, simply make a statement, but don't finish it. Ask your intuition to make the determining declaration for you. For example, if you want to know why a man you have been seeing suddenly refuses to go to the movies with you and your girlfriend (as he has done in the past), you might close your eyes briefly, center yourself, look at the person's forehead, and extend your concentration inward. Then simply say, "He won't go to the movies tonight, because . . . " Give him a mental tap on the head.

Immediately, you "feel" he has had prior problems with your girlfriend, and she tried to come on to him. He's simply not interested but doesn't want to reject her totally and cause problems between you and her. Wow. You never would have guessed it. Now, to see if what you picked up is correct, either suggest that you go alone or that your girlfriend really wants to come, but you'll make sure she brings a date. No reason to explain your decision. See if he relaxes and changes his mind.

Another exercise is to place yourself inside another person's body. "Don't judge a man until you've walked two moons in his moccasins," from the book *Walk Two Moons* by Sharon Creech, is a statement worth remembering. Pretend that you are them; feel what it's like to be them, talking to you. Exercise your perception, and flex your imagination and intellect. What kind of impression are you getting? Keep your own thinking out of it. Start with simple emotions: anger, fear, boredom, envy, happiness, joy, love, confusion, just to touch on a few possibilities. Basically, you want to become them. Ask how you would describe yourself from their perspective. See yourself as they are seeing you. You may be surprised to pick up on subliminal, subconscious impulses that even they aren't consciously aware of.

When a person speaks to you, try to reach out with your mind and touch them. It's more than visualizing; you are actually reaching right inside them and touching their heart. Just borrow a tiny little sample of the energy. Now ask yourself what it feels like. A lot of times, the underlying emotions you pick up, and what you experience physically, are two completely separate entities. When people talk, there's often a hidden message between the words. When they're not talking, there's a hidden message between the silence.

Don't focus on the subject matter, so much as the way it is being transmitted. Watch their demeanor and presentation, especially if you are around exceptionally smart men. They've learned to camouflage their true emotions, shifting it at will to match the color of the mood they wish to express. And what will you receive by doing this? The truth. Hidden emotions, dark shadows, their pain, their fears. This is what you want to see. Not their bodies, or their personalities, but the true essence of the inner person.

Don't worry about infringing on their thoughts. You are only infringing on your own.

SILENT TALKING

When a thought goes off in your mind, whose thought is it? Yours? How can you be one hundred percent certain that it didn't come from somewhere else? We've been brought up to believe that we generate our own thoughts. We've been programmed to believe that. But, maybe, just maybe our thoughts are not as separate as we believe. Think about the power of suggestion. Now what if someone is making the suggestion unconsciously, silently? Doubtful, you say? But how often has this happened to you? You're sitting in a meeting, and daydreaming about something entirely different from the topic at hand. There's a beach, the sun is warm on your flesh, and the water is creeping up to kiss your toes. Suddenly the person next to you says, "I think I might go to Hawaii for my vacation later this year. I don't know why, but Hawaii sounds so good to me right now."

Next time you are with someone you truly care about, but you are afraid to tell them that, say, "I love you," to them in your mind. Watch to see if their lips move into an imperceptible smile. Our brains manipulate energy into intricate patterns of thought in a split millisecond, communicating on a subliminal level. If that's the case, whether silently listening or speaking, what really takes place happens in a place where light is born. Increased sensitivity to the energy of the relationship, while applying the knowledge of body language, can help you understand what a person is feeling. Add to that your intuitive reactions, and you will not only understand what they are feeling but also what they are experiencing.

Whether you realize it or not, you are constantly being fed information. In order to gain control, you must also be able to find the meaning in the messages. You say you don't understand. But your gut, your gizmo, whatever you want to call it does. Read into it the way you read into a horse through his eyes. Charge into an endless green meadow with wisdom and wit running wild and free.

What if you receive negative information? Okay, stop right there. First of all, you cannot assume that anything is good or bad. How would you know? It may not appear to be to your advantage at the moment, but in the overall scheme of things, how would you know? Let's say you're trying to find out if this man is "the one." You want him to be the one because you are head over heels, gaga in love with him, and you're thinking that if he's not a part of your life, you'll just die.

You meditate. You get clear. You focus and get right inside his head. And the only answer you get back is no. A big, fat "NO!" Ain't no way, ain't no how, you imagine the two of you spending your lives together in matrimonial bliss. Not exactly what you wanted to hear, right? If in spiritual reality, everything happens because it is meant to, then this, too, holds meaning.

So, what do you do now? Well, you don't die that's for sure. If you've been paying attention, which I know you have, then you were completely cognizant of the fact that one should never rely entirely upon intuitive information, just as one should never rely entirely upon intellectual information. In both cases, verify. Verify and then verify again. Then think about them inwardly with your heart. Don't force it. In fact, the less you force it the better. You are feeling what you are feeling for a reason. Investigate. Perhaps you got a gut feeling that he's seeing other women, that he's not as serious about the relationship as you are, or maybe he just has commitment issues, or is still looking for someone young and dumb, which would not be you. Should you dump him? Heck no. Should you look into it? Hell yeah! It's time to do some snooping around. I'm not talking about stalking. I am talking about asking the right questions and being aware of his answers.

What if your gut was right? Thank God! I mean it. Wouldn't you rather know now than months down the road? Or worse, what if you turned off the volume on your inner voice completely and actually married the jerk, only to find him cheating on you a few months into the marriage? Losing him could be the best, worst thing that could happen to you. You can now move on and meet the most perfect man in the world for you. Trust the universe on this. If there is a God, and I know there is, he's smarter than you or me.

When an unconscious thought fails to become conscious it appears as fate. May your fate take you to places you never thought you could go.

CONCLUSION–TRANSFORMING YOUR WORLD

The next time you have an important choice to make, whether about a man you intend to marry, or work for, or whatever the case may be, you will be better equipped to make an accurate and sound decision. Not only will you experience uncanny insights into another human being but also into yourself. Understanding how people read you can have a tremendous impact on your life. By applying the same techniques you use to read others, you can fine-tune the impression you are making and literally reinvent yourself.

The first thing I'd like you to do is meet yourself. Unfortunately, our self-perception is not self-formed. Characteristically it is a combination of ideas received from others. Often invalid. So, it's absolutely essential that you be reintroduced with you.

Arrange to be videotaped (preferably in a setting where you are interacting with other people). Professional actors, speakers, and sports players use this technique all the time to improve their game. You, too, can use it to your advantage. Make a note of your posture, your eye contact, and how you are generally coming across. Are the other people involved genuinely interested in what you are saying? Are they sitting close to you, leaning into you, or away from you? What are their facial expressions communicating? Become mindful. Observe yourself.

What kinds of messages are you silently communicating without even realizing it? If your body language is screaming, "I'm not good enough for HIM," then guess what? You're right. I can almost guarantee that you aren't good enough.

What is the number one thing you can do to make yourself physically more attractive? And, I'm not just talking about being more attractive to the opposite sex. I mean to everyone, including yourself. A number ten physique? A perfect complexion? A dynamite wardrobe? If you really want to change how people see you, you have to delve deeper than a superficial level. Temporary fixes will fail you. A deeper level of change is needed, one which involves discovering and then altering our most basic attitudes toward life.

This starts and ends with the energy you emit. Whether you want to admit it or not, it's not so much what you do, as what think that makes you who you are and what you experience. People pick up on your real thoughts, whether you intend for them to or not. It penetrates and permeates a virtual level, which cannot be registered by the five senses—only the sixth and beyond. (I have to believe we possess more than half a dozen.)

The first step in increasing your attractiveness to others is to increase your attractiveness to yourself. Strengthen your own emotional attitudes. Increase your own sense of well-being. Then people will see naturally, from your body language, by the fashion in which your actions follow suit with your words, that you are clothed in a warm and fuzzy security blanket. When they lean, you step back. When they yell, you remain silent. People like controlled strength. It makes them feel safe and supported. It's *attractive*. Subconsciously, they feel your strength and are drawn to it.

You can change who you are. Ray Birdwhistell, a pioneer in the study of body language, indicated that we are taught to be who we end up being. In other words, it is not predetermined. He sites the fact that people in geographical areas will share certain physical traits, albeit they do share genes. The way you sit, the way you talk, the way you smile, the way you laugh, and a million other details of your personal appearance are learned from the people consistently in your life. If this is true, if you learn to be who you are, then you can learn to be someone else.

Unfortunately, a lot of people wait for a traumatic event in their life. A woman who gets a divorce takes matters into her own hand and suddenly loses weight, has her hair done in a more flattering, current style, has some work done on her face, or will buy new cosmetics. Sometimes her whole wardrobe will change. Suddenly she's not running around in frayed caftans anymore. The question is why wait? Become more aware of the way you see the world around you and how you fit in to it. Rather than making you more self-involved, you become more self-invested. Your head will come out of the clouds and in so doing, you will save yourself a lot of grief and disappointment. Not only will this enable you to help yourself but also to help other people. After all, life is your classroom.

Once you feel comfortable with who and what you are, take a minute to stop. Stop and see yourself in your mind's eye. Reach out a hand and say, "Hi, it's really, really nice to meet you."

Now that you've finally met yourself, before you go rushing around searching for the perfect man to marry, why not marry the new you? Buy yourself a ring, a bottle of champagne, flowers for your bouquet; plan what you will wear, and where you will go on your honeymoon (a place you can go to just to love yourself). It need not be complicated or costly. The vacation can be as simple as pampering yourself at a beauty salon. It doesn't matter what it is, as long as you are making love to yourself. Please get your mind out of the gutter, if that's where it went. Shame on you. Now . . .

If this is difficult to do, then imagine yourself stepping out of your own body, walking away from yourself, then turning around to look at . . . who? To look at the magnificent person you are. People having surgery, or near death experiences, often have this same sensation. They rise above their bodies, looking down at what happened to them. You don't have to be close to death to understand how this works. You can simply imagine yourself doing the same thing. Stand in front of a mirror and have a real ceremony. I mean it. Make a commitment to your own inner journey in transforming yourself into the best person you can be without the help of anyone else (except the spiritual force within you). Say aloud, "Do you take this person to be your lawful wedded self? To have and to hold, for better, for worse . . . "

You'll be amazed at how good you feel afterwards. You love you. Searching for a soul mate to complete you, to be the other half of you, will no longer suffice. Half a person will find another half a person, and they will still be in search of another whole. Two whole people, however, will find happiness and joy.

It's sad to say, but relationships have a built-in possibility not to last. Why? When you accentuate love, you are in fact accentuating yourself. You open yourself up to your vulnerabilities. All of your fears, your destructive tendencies, and bad habits become amplified. In a superficial relationship, you can hide your defenselessness, especially with sex. But with someone you love, with whom you become intimate, you can't. You are susceptible. All the excess baggage you carry around will be opened up by the customs officer of your heart and scrutinized to death. If the interrogation doesn't kill you, you'll be the happiest person alive.

Body language is about self-awareness, which in turn should lead to self-development and, ultimately, personal growth. It is not about manipulating people. You can try that, but it generally backfires more than my first car. That's because it's unnatural to begin with. If you are consciously altering your image to gain control in a situation, you are not being true to yourself. A man may pretend to be generous and kind, and will probably attract a lot of women in doing so, but chances are, on the second or third date his true colors come shining through like that of the used car with the Earl Shrive paint job.

And what happens if the relationship becomes serious? I don't think so. A huge yawn in the earth is where one falls, doomed to endlessly tumble through the precipitous void frequently referred to as being something you are not. As Abraham Lincoln said, "You can fool some of the people some of the time, but you can't fool all of the people all of time." Please don't fool yourself.

By now, you have gained tremendous insight into people. Hopefully, the techniques in this book will be used to understand, not to manipulate, them. I am not going to get into what is karmically correct here, as that would be abstract and prosaic. My goal was to help you embark on your own journey of self-discovery, for if you read other people, you can read yourself. The only way you become a better person is through other people. That's how you discover yourself, that's how you express yourself and uncover the true nature of your being.

Find yourself. Find love.

RECOMMENDED READING

De Becker, Gavin, *The Gift of Fear*, New York, Dell Publishing, 1997

Birdwhistell, Raymond, *Kinesics and Context*, New York, Penguin Publishing, 1973

Bolting, Kate, *Sex Appeal*, New York, St. Martin's Press, 1993.

Davies, Rodney, *How to Read Faces*, Wellingborough, England, Thorsons Publishing Group, Aquarian Press, 1989.

Dimitrious, Jo Ellan, and Mark Mazzarella, *Reading People*, New York, Random House, 1998.

Fast, Julius, *Body Language*, New York, Pocket Books, 1970.

Ekman, Paul, *Telling Lies: Cues to Deceit in the Marketplace, Politics and Marriage*, New York, W. W. Norton and Company, 1985.

Ekman, Paul and W.V. Friesen, *Unmasking the Face*, Englewood Cliffs, N.J., Prentice-Hall, 1975.

Glass, Lillian, *I Know What You're Thinking: Using the Four Codes of Reading People to Improve Your Life*, New York, John Wiley & Sons, 2002.

Hall, Calvin S. and Vernon, J. Nordby, *A Primer of Jungian Psychology*, New York, Penguin, The New American Library, Inc., 1973.

Lieberman, David J., *Never Be Lied to Again*, New York, St. Martin's Press, 1998.

Nance, Jef, *Conquering Deception*, Kansas City, Irvin-Benham Group, LLC, 2002.

Nierenberg, Gerald I., and Henry H. Calero, *How to Read a Person Like a Book*, New York: Pocket Books, 1971.

Steele, R. Don, *Body Language Secrets: A Guide During Courtship and Dating*, Whittier, Ca., Steel Balls Press, 1997.

Tieger, Paul D., and Barbara Barron Tieger, *The Art of Speed Reading People*, Boston, Little Brown Company, 1998.

Wainright, Gordon R., *Body Language*, Chicago, NTC Publishing Group, 1985.

HOW TO CONTACT THE AUTHOR

For additional information on seminars and lectures write to:

Servet Hasan
Post Office Box 1209
Lake Forest, California 92609-1209

Or e-mail her at:
servet@HasWil.com

Printed in the United States
20944LVS00001BC/205